Praise for

THE BIBLE AS IMPROV

Ron Martoia is a deep and elegant thinker and a clear and engaging writer. Not only do I love what he writes, but I've had the chance to see him in action, leading groups and creating space for people to think, learn, discover, and grow. Reading this book feels like being in a group facilitated by Ron, so I know it will help people rediscover the Bible and find their place in its ongoing, life-transforming, world-changing drama.

> BRIAN D. MCLAREN, author/speaker *brianmclaren.net*

A welcome introduction to new and alternative ways of understanding and living out the script of Christian faith. Ron Martoia offers fresh perspectives for the ongoing task of interpreting the Bible in the midst of an ever-changing world and invites readers to participate in the ongoing story of God's mission in ways that are both faithful and innovative.

> JOHN R. FRANKE, the Clemens professor of missional theology
> at Biblical Seminary in Hatfield, Pennsylvania,
> and author of *Manifold Witness*

Surely the Bible, of all books, ought to stimulate serious dialogue. If it doesn't, we should wonder whether it is being read properly. Ron provides us a completely unconventional and deliciously controversial look into how we interpret Scripture, or rather, how we allow it to interpret us.

> ALAN HIRSCH, author of *The Forgotten Ways*
> and coauthor of *Untamed* (with Debra Hirsch)

This book will change the way you read The Book.

> MARK BATTERSON, lead pastor of National Community Church
> and author of *In a Pit with a Lion on a Snowy Day*

Ron is scary smart. He sees things that most of us don't see. And yet in the midst of his sheer brilliance, he is able to communicate in such a practical and engaging way. *The Bible as Improv* is a perfect example of why when Ron has something to say, I pay close attention.

Mike Foster, creative principal at PlainJoe Studios

If you have ever witnessed a jazz ensemble breathe fresh life into a classic Miles Davis piece, then you have a sense of what Ron Martoia is inviting us to through *The Bible as Improv*. Faithfulness and playfulness dancing together toward fullness of life, immersion in the history of the art, keen awareness of prior interpretations, skillful use of one's instrument, thoughtful study of the charts, interpreters playing off one another in community and with the audience. *The Bible as Improv* is a beautiful exercise in practical biblical hermeneutics.

Dwight J. Friesen, associate professor of practical theology at Mars Hill Graduate School in Seattle, Washington, and author of *Thy Kingdom Connected*

Ron Martoia in this delightfully well-written book invites us into a new, conjunctive stage of faith where paradox, society, and God can exist in peaceful tension. From a new vantage point where the Bible is no longer viewed as an owner's manual to make everything hum but as a classic, we are challenged to live the biblical text through new conversations we engage in with the text. The jazz metaphor serves as another helpful image to convey the meaning of the dance of improv, where the Bible becomes the score that we, in the company of other Jesus-followers, immerse ourselves in. In this way the Bible comes alive through the music we are making with our lives. This masterful book by a modern-day prophet in blue jeans opens up fresh pathways for all who wish to replace their dated reading maps of the Bible.

Stephan Joubert, extraordinary professor of New Testament studies, University of Pretoria, South Africa, and editor echurch/ekerk

THE BIBLE AS IMPROV

Seeing & Living the Script in New Ways

RON MARTOIA

ZONDERVAN.com/
AUTHORTRACKER
follow your favorite authors

ZONDERVAN

The Bible as Improv
Copyright © 2010 by Ron Martoia

This title is also available as a Zondervan ebook.
Visit www.zondervan.com/ebooks.

This title is also available in a Zondervan audio edition.
Visit www.zondervan.fm.

Requests for information should be addressed to:

Zondervan, *Grand Rapids, Michigan 49530*

Library of Congress Cataloging-in-Publication Data

Martoia, Ron, 1962–
    The Bible as improv : seeing and living the script in new ways / Ron Martoia.
      p. cm.
    Includes bibliographical references.
    ISBN 978-0-310-28770-4 (softcover)
    1. Bible — Criticism, interpretation, etc. 2. Christian life. 3. Christian
biography. I. Title.
    BS511.3.M327 2009
    220.6 – dc22
                                      2009018558

Published in association with the literary agency of Daniel Literary Group, LLC,
1701 Kingsbury Drive, Suite 100, Nashville, TN 37215.

Interior design: Melissa Elenbaas

Printed in the United States of America

10 11 12 13 14 15 16 • 22 21 20 19 18 17 16 15 14 13 12 11 10 9 8 7 6 5 4 3 2 1

TO TY JAMES—

A first son
A first grandson
A first great-grandson
A first great-great-grandson

CONTENTS

PART 3 | Improv-ing the Script:
Learning to Riff in Community

ACKNOWLEDGMENTS

MUCH OF THE stimulus for this book came out of the deep questions I have had about the Bible since my high school days. But the truth is that several faith communities I have been part of over the past twenty years have fueled and tweaked my questions, raised new ones of their own, and contributed extended dialogue on the subject in gracious and heartfelt ways. These faith communities and a number of conversation partners are the ultimate impetus to this volume.

Spiritual Explorations Live, Ted Baird's Fellowship Church @ Anthem's learning nights, and our theology staff days with Joe Lengel at Waterville Community Church have all contributed to the ideas in the book. Using Velocityculture.com's III:Text seminary-like learning containers, we just completed a module (III:Text.4) on the biblical text where we talked about many of the questions posed here. The conversation was stimulating, intelligent, illuminating, and warm. I thank all of you for being such a great sounding board and for engaging in such genuine dialogue.

I can't help but mention a few of my conversation partners. Christian McCabe at New Providence Community Church in Nassau is a deep personal friend and a voice I love to hear. His ability to alchemically grab previously disparate streams and to synthesize them into a compelling whole is really without equal. I continue to be fueled by his great questions, new angles, and sometimes startling observations. Christian, thank you for your life, voice, and heart. More times on the horizon with you and Nicole.

Scott Mawdesley is a stimulating and thoughtful champion for deeper reflection and an intentional listener. We don't connect nearly enough, but when we do, it is stellar. For your and Natalie's friendship, encouragement, and support, I thank you, my friend.

I am reminded how encouraging Brian McLaren has been to my life in general and my writing pursuits in particular as he sat in my living room this week and talked with me into the morning hours about the Bible. For the last several years, we have had the opportunity to interface in the ups and downs of life in which God has to live large in our lives. I am grateful for his stimulating thoughts and perspectives and for being one of those balcony people in my life.

Joe Tessin is a comrade-in-arms who has courageously taken God at his word and carries out an amazing ministry in Georgia. Our conversations over the past year during the writing of this book have been heartwarming and forced me to think about how to communicate some of these ideas more clearly and succinctly (not sure, though, how well I listened). Thanks, Joe, for your friendship and verbal sparring.

I also acknowledge several key professorial voices that have molded me, for better or for worse, when it comes to my reading of the Bible: Dr. Arden Autry, Dr. Siegfried Schatzmann, Dr. John Sailhamer, and Dr. Scot McKnight. I owe Scot a debt of gratitude for an introduction he made not long after my graduation from a master's program in which he was my adviser. At a Society of Biblical Literature meeting, Scot invited me ("a former student") to grab coffee with him and a professor friend of his. I wouldn't know the value of that introduction for several years—because when Scot introduced me to Tom Wright, I hadn't the slightest idea who he was. Years later, I would come to realize the value of that meeting and of the indelible mark Professor Wright would make on me and on the content of this book.

PART 1

MY JOURNEY WITH THE SCRIPTURE SCRIPT

The Good, the Bad, and the Inconsistent

The first few years of my life with the Bible were formative for reasons you are about to discover. Our initial experience with the text of the Bible and the viewpoints we are exposed to through those first teachers are indelible markings in our lives. Some of those markings are tattoos we dearly love, telling a story of an exhilarating journey with the Word of God. Some of those markings are scars we would love to have surgically removed, and they will mark our journeys forever. Whatever the case, my love for God's Word — a love that continues to this day — was forged in those early experiences and biblical encounters that mark me for better or for worse.

I hope you can get in touch with how your approach to God's Word has been formed, so that you can more adequately see if your current approach serves you well and the God to whom it points.

Changing our view of the Bible or our view of God has an immediate impact on the other. Let's explore this idea together.

ONE

CHAPTER

MY FIRST EXPERIENCE

Reading the Bible for Principles for Life

DIRT WAS FLYING as I heard a sickening snap followed by a thud. Not a good sound as I slid into second base. The snap was an ankle, the thud my foot finally reaching the bag. It was the top of the first inning, it was opening day, and I was batting cleanup. But that audible crack was an almost certain indication I wasn't going to be pitching on *this* first-game day.

I had worked with coaches all preseason long to ensure that this final year of senior league ball would see my best pitching performances ever. Of course, at the mature age of fifteen, you have pretty keen expectations: With a little effort, a full-ride college scholarship would be forthcoming because you are so close to being pro caliber. At this moment, however, I wasn't too concerned about college offers. I was in pain—physical pain due to my broken ankle, but deeper emotional pain due to the loss of my ability to play my senior year of league competition—putting my hope of professional pitching into jeopardy.

Little did I know this was to be a turning point, the first of many to come.

Earlier that same year, in the middle of January, in the dead of winter, my mom had decided to take me to a Bible fellowship meeting composed predominantly of women. I was the child of a mixed marriage: a Presbyterian mom and a Catholic dad. When you do the math, you can see this isn't a very fun scenario. One traditional Presby and one traditional Catholic added up to two church services every Sunday for me and my two younger brothers. We started the trek at 10:30 at the Presbyterian church and followed that up with the 12:00 guitar Mass at St. John's or St. Mary's. Jeanette's Diner was the weekly place of choice where my brothers and I could finally exhale and relax.

This wasn't enough for my mom though. She had gotten bit by the Bible study bug. She started attending a study some months earlier, and it really changed her. I could see it, and so could my dad. So when she asked, I decided to go along. This particular Saturday in January, a man was coming to talk about the Bible and the power of the Holy Spirit. I don't have the slightest idea what this guy's name was, where he was from, or what he did the other six days a week when he wasn't speaking on Saturday to small groups of women who wore too much perfume. I do know he made an impression on me about how God actually speaks to us through his Word, the Bible—and how we ought to take this truth seriously. That message stuck in my head—but, to be honest, only in my head. I didn't have a flash of motivation to start reading or studying the Bible, and I certainly didn't "desire the Word."

I hadn't thought about that snowy January morning since, and had never attended another study with my mom. But that warm May night on the ball field set in motion a series of events that would forever change my life.

As fate—or, as I would now say, God—would have it, Mom's monthly Bible study happened to fall on the Saturday morning of the same week of the broken ankle event. When Mom got home at noon on Saturday, she had some news for me: "Your leg is healed." She made the announcement with a straight face and total seriousness as she decided to call our *Jewish* family-friend—a bone specialist—to meet us at the hospital to cut off the cast.

I was shocked and elated all at the same time, and to be honest I never even questioned the veracity of my mom's claim. Sounded good to me. My Mensa member dad wasn't quite as gung ho. I think skeptical (at best) is a fair assessment as he tried to dissuade Mom from doing anything too rash or, let's be honest, embarrassing. My mom's Bible study group was a charismatic women's fellowship with groups that met all over the United States. Praying for physical healing and "trusting God's Word" were what they did every month when they got together.

So off to the hospital we went. The doctor was not too excited. His Saturday afternoon was being interrupted by a friend who, as far as he could tell, had gone off the religious deep end. I remember expletives and words about "I'm doing this as a favor, but this might be about the most ridiculous request I've heard in a long time."

His posture did not remain hostile long, however. His countenance quickly turned to incredulity as he cut away the cast, ordered a rotation of X-rays (taken for the second time in four days), and then scanned the report from the radiologist: the long break running from my ankle up into my shin was only faintly visible and was clearly filled in. In comparison to three days earlier, it was obvious, even to an untrained eye, that something dramatic had occurred. "Total bewilderment" is a good description of my doc's state of mind.

He wasn't comfortable in giving me the "all clear" without having other doctors weigh in on the phenomenon. So I was put in a walking cast for a few days until a couple other doctors could review reports and X-ray my leg (for yet a third time). The result? What was supposed to be a ten- to twelve-week ordeal ended in nine days. Clean bill of health.

God had showed up in nothing short of a miraculous way. Life changing? Yes. Trajectory altering? Indeed. The full extent of what this healing meant, however, would take a number of months to emerge.

A dramatic physical healing is an attention getter for anyone. For me it was a ticket back to summer stardom — or so I thought. I figured I would be back on the team for Monday practice and back to pitching in short order. God had other plans. My coach had removed me from the roster the day after I broke my ankle and drafted another guy for the team. He had to fill the spot. The excitement I had about rejoining the team gave way to even greater disappointment. My summer pitching possibilities were gone — long gone. "This is going to be the longest summer on record," I thought to myself. "What in the world am I going to do?"

Something had already happened inside me. I wanted to understand why in the world God would heal me and then "remove" baseball from my life. What came flooding back to me were the words of the man who spoke on that shivering cold morning inside the Holiday Inn banquet room. "God speaks to us through his Word; he really does."

That week, I went to our local Christian bookstore, Agape, where the local bookstore owner pointed me to the Living Bible — a relatively new paraphrase he said was perfect for getting into the Bible, and especially good for young people. This one had a green padded cover, and so I bought it. I had been given other Bibles before. My Presbyterian confirmation pastor had placed in my hands a black leather Revised Standard Version Bible. I remember from my childhood the children's Bibles out of which my folks would read us Bible stories. But this Living Bible was the first personal "study" Bible through which I would come to test the assertion that God speaks to us through the Bible.

This was my first encounter of the mesmerizing power of Scripture and the big story of God. My summer was spent, not playing ball, but reading the Bible through from beginning to end. I couldn't stop reading. I started with the hope of finding answers to: Why no more baseball? In a couple of weeks, though, I had stopped asking the question and had gotten enthralled in a story far bigger than summer baseball. Something was happening as I entered a whole new world.

While many of the biblical stories were familiar, the pace and tempo of reading the stories in sequence and in large blocks had a totally different effect on me from that of the "one Bible story a week" experience I had at my mom's church, or the spliced-up lectionary readings of my dad's.

I still have that Bible, dressed with a thick-vinyl blue iridescent cover trimmed in brown—complete with replica Bible coins on a grosgrain ribbon bookmark. (I had been fully initiated into the world of Bible gear and individual marking techniques.) I thumbed through it the other day, looking at all my markings and notes in the margins, and it made me smile to see what happened in the early days of my personal journey. Whenever I see that Bible, I remember what a catalytic, life-changing summer that was. God used my "tragedy" as the life shift I needed to be introduced to a whole new playing field that was a lot bigger than a ball diamond.

YEAH, HE DID SPEAK

I am sure my foray into the biblical world is no more unique than most. I realized that truth then, and I have an even greater appreciation now for the ways in which God leads his people to his Word. How much my broken leg, disappointment, and quest for "the answer" fueled the experience is hard to calculate; but the facts of falling in love with reading God's Word and the resulting transformation are beyond dispute. God was unmistakably speaking. I didn't hear voices in my head. I did, however, have this growing purpose, this dawning that God was giving me a new point of reference.

Not only did I read the entire Bible cover to cover, but by the time I began my junior year of high school a few months later, I had read numerous Bible study books and wanted to share my Bible reading insights with others. My excitement fueled an effort to see my discoveries have an impact on other people.

And that is exactly what happened. My junior year was an interesting time of self-discovery, spiritual growth, leadership development, and incredible life change. I had been converted, or was being converted — or was at least in the process of change. I heard something several years later that was true of me at this stage: "Anyone who has had a spiritual experience ought to be locked up and gagged for six months until they can figure out how to explain or articulate what has happened to them without offending every living, breathing creature within earshot." I am sure I offended more people than I helped during my junior year, but there were a few, a growing few, who got bit by the God bug; and for them, that year of high school was nothing short of transformative.

Our entry into Bible exposure and the resulting knowledge we gain have a lot to do with how we end up feeling about the Bible for the rest of our lives. If you come from a background where the Bible was used as a rule book to beat you into submission, your experience will be jaded. If you had absolutely no Bible exposure until you were thirty-two years old, your experience may be quite exciting. I know that my first taste was quite positive. For that I am thankful because it has colored everything for me; it has had a dramatic impact on every area of my life for thirty years. And it has colored my friends too.

THE TATTOO INCIDENT

Applying Leviticus 19 by Picking and Choosing

MY FIRST COUPLE of years of immersion in God's Word were formative years—formative not only because of my increased exposure to the Bible, but because I encountered the first difficult conundrums with the book during my remaining high school years. I suspect that most people exposed to the Bible as a child or teen come to it with a naïveté reflecting an age-appropriate development. In other words, at age fifteen, when I started reading the Bible, and having been exposed to it since birth, I had a tacit assumption that the Bible was true.

On the surface, such a statement seems to be a simple, easy-to-grasp assertion, but several implicit assumptions accompany this little statement. Where I grew up, even in my Presbyterian/Catholic mix, the Bible as true meant the stories were true, that is, they were historical, verifiable facts. Furthermore, since it was true, it was to be applied to life. *All* of it applied to *all* of life. I don't remember this ever being explicitly taught to me, but I do remember Bible study books from my early impressionable years that would quote a passage such as Joshua 1:6–9:

> Be strong and courageous, because you will lead these people to inherit the land I swore to their ancestors to give them.
>
> Be strong and very courageous. Be careful to obey all the law my servant Moses gave you; do not turn from it to the right or to the left, that you may be successful wherever you go. Keep this Book of the Law always on your lips; meditate on it day and night, so that you may be careful to do everything written in it. Then you will be prosperous and successful. Have I not commanded you? Be strong and courageous. Do not be afraid; do not be discouraged, for the LORD your God will be with you wherever you go.

A passage such as this one might be quoted in a Bible study book to prod the recognition that *every word* in the Bible is important — and an obedient response to *all of it* would ensure that my young life would come to great success and prosperity.

I remember reading Joshua for the first time and thinking, "This is the key to all of life and success." I wrote these verses on an index card — a card, incidentally, I recently found as I went through an old box looking for that first Bible I had purchased. This was going to be my "life verse," the passage that would mark my discipline and my focus on the Bible's impact on my life and future. The Bible as true meant it was to be *applied to all of life*.

Nothing seemed crazy, out of sync, or extreme in thinking that the words given directly to Joshua also applied directly to me. Never once did it occur to me that I was doing something inappropriate or that I was mishandling the Bible by making this jump. You may be thinking the very same thing. *Of course* the Bible is true. *Of course* all of it applies to all of life. And *of course* the word given to Joshua is just as applicable to me as it was to him. This I have come to find out is a normal and natural stage of development.

That posture seems to work fine until . . .

SUNDAY NIGHT BIBLE STUDY

During the fall after my summer of discovery of the Bible, I really wanted to share my faith. I wanted to help my friends fall in love with the Bible, as I had. My folks allowed me to host a few friends at our house for a Sunday night Bible study.

Keith was one of the first guys I invited into "Study," as it came to be called—and he came to investigate. Keith was a great friend. I learned to water-ski on the lake by his cottage, and we hung out together at different times during the summer. Several other guys and gals joined us for those first six to eight months. We learned a lot together.

I invited them into the only thing I knew to do: cherry-pick passages that seemed important to me, explain what I thought they meant, then open the floor for discussion. The blind leading the blind would be a more than generous description of what was going on.

Joshua 1 seemed far more important than the death of Moses and his inability to get into the Promised Land (recounted in Deuteronomy 34), so in our initial Sunday night meetings, we focused on those types of passages.

I amped-up my knowledge by using a concordance.[1] That fall, I was doing searches on keywords and then stringing those passages together in some sort of funky pastiche, and we were becoming students of the Word of God! Those were the days of unfettered trust, ease of Bible use, and certainty about our understanding of the Bible.

That was all about to change. Our shared naïveté was about to get a wake-up call and jolt us into the real world.

Several months into Study, Keith announced he wanted to ask a question and see if we could do a Bible study around it. Keith had decided he wanted to get a tattoo. Now let me frame this a bit. Except in the most conservative circles today, tattoos aren't even a conversation to be undertaken biblically; but back then, it was a big deal. Keith's mom wasn't a bit happy about this idea. She expressed her displeasure by insisting that only war veterans and motorcycle gang members had tattoos. She then trumped all arguments Keith might have offered by quoting Leviticus 19:28: "Do not cut your bodies for the dead or put tattoo marks on yourselves. I am the LORD."

Keith was bummed out but not dissuaded. Something didn't seem totally right to him—or to the rest of us, for that matter—about that verse. He just couldn't believe it applied to him. Of course, for the previous several months we had been building a pretty hard and fast case that if the Bible said it, you had to do it. We had no other framework to consider.

So here was my first initiation into biblical interpretation dilemmas and my first experience with how the Bible could be used to attempt to control people's behavior—both of which were merely "firsts." What I came to realize very quickly was that not only would we face many interpretation dilemmas, but that many people viewed the Bible as the ultimate behavior control mechanism. In some ways I totally understood this, since I, too, believed that if the Bible said it, that settled it. This didn't seem like control at the time, but rather simply being faithful to God and what he had revealed as his will.

That night, we got out the concordance; and though we were using a variety of Bible versions, the text in Leviticus was clear: no marks, no tattoos. At this stage in our development, we hadn't even realized there were other questions that might be important to ask, such as, "What does the rest of the passage teach?" "Who was this written to?" "If the passage is in the Old Testament, does it still apply today?" Since we could find no other passages of Scripture about tattooing, the conversation moved toward all of us weighing in on what we saw as the pros and cons of tats. I realize now, in hindsight, just how important that shift was. When we have no other framework from which to read a text, we will automatically resort to doing what comes naturally, namely, stating our opinion and preference.

The problem, of course, was that no one was satisfied with our opinions on the topic. We had already studied enough of the Bible to know that our personal outlooks on any topic had to be guided by the Bible. And just because we didn't like the tattoo passage and what it meant for Keith didn't mean we could ignore it. The Bible was the final authority and the last word on any topic.

But the last word *hadn't* been spoken.

Tara was a sharp gal who had been coming to Study for just a couple of months. She was from an Assembly of God background and seemed to have more Bible knowledge than all the others combined. Right after our opening prayer, as we were getting ready to dive in to our Bible study the following week, she started the conversation with some questions: "Do all of you stand when someone older than you enters a room? Have you ever had any concerns about getting a haircut—or for the few of you guys who might be mature enough to shave, any concerns about that?" We all laughed at the "mature" comment and the shaving idea. All of the guys could point to three or four wild, inch-long hairs we would let grow on the end of our chins so we could shave every fourth day and claim, "Of course I shave! Are you kidding me?"

As Tara fired away, I was thinking these were pretty random questions; but we volleyed her questions around, laughed, and agreed that we don't stand when someone from our parents' generation walks into the room, nor do we care about haircuts and shaving.

She nodded and went on. "Or how about this? Let's look at the tag in the shirts we're wearing." She reached over her neck and pulled up a tag. "What is your shirt made out of?" We looked at shirt tags and found cotton, rayon, cotton/poly blends, and other material with names we had never heard of.

Tara looked at us and said, "I think we need to go back and continue the conversation from last week, because if the tattoo passage applies to Keith, then we can't get our hair cut or trim our beards, and we have to stand up in the presence of older people — oh, and not to mention that we need to wear clothing that is 100 percent of something — *not* a blend."

We decided we better do some more reading:

> "Keep my decrees.
>
> "Do not mate different kinds of animals.
>
> "Do not plant your field with two kinds of seed.
>
> "Do not wear clothing woven of two kinds of material.
>
> "If a man sleeps with a female slave who is promised to another man but who has not been ransomed or given her freedom, there must be due punishment. Yet they are not to be put to death, because she had not been freed. The man, however, must bring a ram to the entrance to the tent of meeting for a guilt offering to the LORD. With the ram of the guilt offering the priest is to make atonement for him before the LORD for the sin he has committed, and his sin will be forgiven.
>
> "When you enter the land and plant any kind of fruit tree, regard its fruit as forbidden. For three years you are to consider it forbidden; it must not be eaten. In the fourth

year all its fruit will be holy, an offering of praise to the LORD. But in the fifth year you may eat its fruit. In this way your harvest will be increased. I am the LORD your God.

"Do not eat any meat with the blood still in it.

"Do not practice divination or seek omens.

"Do not cut the hair at the sides of your head or clip off the edges of your beard.

"Do not cut your bodies for the dead or put tattoo marks on yourselves. I am the LORD.

"Do not degrade your daughter by making her a prostitute, or the land will turn to prostitution and be filled with wickedness.

"Observe my Sabbaths and have reverence for my sanctuary. I am the LORD.

"Do not turn to mediums or seek out spiritists, for you will be defiled by them. I am the LORD your God.

"Stand up in the presence of the aged, show respect for the elderly and revere your God. I am the LORD."

LEVITICUS 19:19–32

We went back and read the whole chapter—not just the one verse we had read the previous week, the one Keith had given us that had been quoted to him by his mom. We all looked at each other a bit puzzled and confused. What do you do with this passage? How do you sort out the stuff that applies and the stuff that doesn't? I had heard "observe the Sabbath" injunctions my whole life. For crying out loud, I was doing church twice a Sunday at different places. And I had always been told we are to be quiet and reflective in the church, which shows "reverence for [the Lord's] sanctuary" (verse 30). But if verse 30 applies—and according to Keith's mom, it surely does—so does verse 28 (about tattooing), verse 27 (about hair and beard cutting), and verse 19 (about wearing fabric of mixed fibers).

To make matters even more complicated, in the midst of a hot and heavy discussion Tara was quick to point out the last verse of Leviticus 19: "Keep all my decrees and all my laws and follow them. I am the LORD" (verse 37).

We were all committed to the Word of God—and to *all* of the Word of God. But this final line in the last verse of that chapter? This was nothing short of baffling. How in the world do you keep all the decrees listed here? How are you supposed to follow them all? We all realized, even given our immature and undeveloped approach to the Bible, that this was the Old Testament. We understood that Jesus had come and brought a new covenant that superseded the old covenant. We also had discussed the fact that Leviticus as a book was talking about stuff that was largely superseded in the act of Jesus' death on the cross. All the regulations about sacrifices—the how, where, when, and what of it all—was obviously not applicable to those of us who weren't engaged in the sacrificial system.

But what about these other commands that weren't about sacrifice? Do these other ones somehow still have force, or can all of it simply be called "cultural"?

So, in the middle of these discussions, we for the first time flirted with what would become an inescapable and thorny problem. These commands in Leviticus weren't actually written to us; they were written to other people in a different time and place. Of course, this is to state the obvious, but it did raise a confusing and enormously important question—although at that age and stage we didn't know just how enormous: How does stuff written to other people and in other time periods and for other cultures apply to us?

After several weeks of discussion, we came to a tentative conclusion: The Bible is the Word of God, and so it has application far beyond the original group it was written to. What this conclusion didn't solve was the pick-and-choose problem we had identified in Leviticus. What do we pick from that chapter to apply, and what don't we have to worry about? Interestingly, this question is similar to one I still struggle with, and it penetrates to the heart of the problem many people have with the Bible and the church in general: What about our tendency to selectively pick and choose what we like to apply?

The challenges raised in those weeks weren't soon put to bed. Over the next months, we identified all sorts of application issues we were either confused about or simply had no idea how to answer. The confusion came into real focus when Dean, one of my closest friends, who was amazingly intellectual, questioned the application of Joshua 1:6–9, the passage I was in the habit of referring to. None of us ever questioned whether or not we should meditate on the Book of the Law day and night, or whether doing so was a critical component of our being "prosperous and successful" wherever we were to go, a la Joshua.

But Dean threw a wrench in that confidence. His questions were as probing as they were haunting for those of us in Study. Dean's question was simple: "How does a passage written to a guy who is leading a group of former slaves into a promised new home apply to us?" How does God's command to Joshua to meditate on the Book of the Law — the Mosaic law, as Dean was quick to point out — apply to us teenagers? Leviticus, after all, was part of a larger five-book unit called "the Book of the Law" or "the Pentateuch," and we weren't at all sure how large portions of it applied. We had come to an interesting place in our journey, a place that would become a constant companion to this very day.

For the next several months, we continued on in Study and realized there were lots of "tattoo-type" passages. We encountered passages in which certain parts seemed easy enough to apply and others seemed simply inappropriate, unfair, or only applicable to *them back there*—the phrase we began to use to telegraph our thought that "it simply doesn't apply to us now."

THE MASTER VERSE OF THEM ALL

The tattoo weeks were a turning point at Study—and a turning point in my naïveté. I realized you couldn't just read this book and then mechanically apply all of it. The Bible is more complicated, and apparently more confusing, than I first assumed. How to pick and choose—that was the question. Or that was what we thought the question was.

An ensuing week made the pick-and-choose question even more acute. Because we were all young in faith, I would often gravitate toward teaching and discussing passages that had clear relevance and easy application. One of our favorite passages was from the letter to Titus:

> Similarly, encourage the young men to be self-controlled. In everything set them an example by doing what is good. In your teaching show integrity, seriousness and soundness of speech that cannot be condemned, so that those who oppose you may be ashamed because they have nothing bad to say about us.
>
> TITUS 2:6–8

How can you not feel as a high schooler that these verses were written to you? The guys in the Study made this section of Titus a constant conversation piece. The next two verses, however, we had never really thought about:

Teach slaves to be subject to their masters in everything, to try to please them, not to talk back to them, and not to steal from them, but to show that they can be fully trusted, so that in every way they will make the teaching about God our Savior attractive.

TITUS 2:9 – 10

Was this support of slavery back then OK? And if so, how do we justify this? And if it wasn't OK, then why didn't God say something in his Word about it? Why remain mute on such a huge topic having to do with civil rights and the equality of all human beings? Why not simply say, "Hey, Christians, you can't have slaves!"

Finally we got to a passage I thought would put to rest the challenges we had encountered. On the docket for that particular week was a verse that made an observation about *all* Bible verses:

All Scripture is God-breathed and is useful for teaching, rebuking, correcting and training in righteousness, so that all God's people may be thoroughly equipped for every good work.

2 TIMOTHY 3:16 – 17

We knew we had to take the Bible literally or else we would simply be playing fast and loose with the text. Either all of it applies, or none of it applies. Here was our proof that *all* of the Bible was for our training, teaching, and correcting. This passage was the master verse, if you will, the granddaddy of them all. Who were we to pick and choose what applied and did not apply? The first part of 2 Timothy 3:16 says *all Scripture* — not some, not the convenient parts, not the parts we would like to apply — but *all* Scripture was God-breathed and therefore useful.

But ...

There was always the "but." Enlightenment about a passage such as this one didn't clarify our Leviticus 19 dilemma. Sure, we all bought without reservation the idea that the whole Bible was for our teaching and training. But how does it all apply? Was I forbidden to wear my marching band uniform because it was a mixed fiber garment of cotton and polyester? (I checked.)

What we began kicking around was the idea that one Bible verse or passage cannot be used to trump another passage or force it to do something. We were wrestling with *how* the Bible is used for our training, not the issue of if all of it should be. We did not question if Leviticus was included in the Bible for some purpose. The question was, For *what* purpose? And so went our Ping-Pong understanding. We would read a master verse such as 2 Timothy 3:16 and then stumble onto a passage that just didn't seem to apply to us. Back and forth we went. One thing was clear: we were confused. We were definitely at an impasse in our understanding.

PRESBYTERIAN, CATHOLIC, AND CHARISMATIC

Wearing Lenses

MY BIBLICAL DILEMMAS were not quickly solved, but my enthusiasm remained, and I continued to be excited and engaged in Bible study, memorization, and meditation. A growing number of friends were coming to Study every week in my family room, and the excitement of growing with God and wanting to make a difference was very real. To say we experienced a minirevival might be an overstatement, but to say our lives were being dramatically changed would be dead-on. Kids were no longer coming home on Friday nights hammered; Saturday night curfews seemed intact all of a sudden—and parents were the first to notice. These were interesting days in my development and in my understanding of how to "use" the Bible.

I now recognize that the "certainty value" was ingrained very early in my Christian development—a value held high in the modern church world. We love knowing we are right and take it as an implicit mandate to get others on our "correct" page. Years later, I am not convinced that certainty, on the one hand, and knowing and experiencing God, on the other, are good bedfellows. Nor do I think the Bible was given to us for the purpose of certainty. But it took quite a biblical and personal journey for me to arrive at this conclusion.

PERFUME AND INDELIBLE MARKS

I was walking down the street in Scottsdale, Arizona, when we were in town to drop off our number two son, Skyler, at Arizona State University. Out of nowhere I caught a whiff of a perfume that instantly took me back to my college days and a certain girlfriend. I vividly remembered a picnic on a hot, sunny day, having a good time playing Frisbee and eating cheese and bread with my girlfriend on a big blanket. I hadn't thought of her in years. The perfume scent I caught some twenty years later was either the same perfume or something so similar that I was instantly transported.

Have you ever had that happen? Scent is a powerfully anchored sense. The smell of certain types of food might remind you of Grandma's house or of a special restaurant. My Italian grandpa made his own wine every season. He gave all the grandkids their very own shot glass of dago red wine almost every time we would visit (until he ran out and we had to wait for next season). Whenever I catch that scent, I'm transported back to Grandpa Martoia's house and its thick cigar smoke, dago red, and homemade pasta fagioli.

Early experiences leave indelible markings, even markings on the formation of our worldview. Those etchings have a domino effect on how we view everything. You pick the topic or event — first day of school, first baseball game, first ballet recital, first kiss. Any one of them illustrates the truth. Our first teachings about God and handling of the Bible are no different. Early experiences are powerful shapers, but we often don't realize how powerful they are until we can step outside of the influence long enough to see it with new eyes.

DOES IT PREACH IN PEORIA AND PUNJAB?

In my childhood, I was taught that God had established the world on a pretty clear cause-and-effect model: You reap what you sow.[1] I mentioned my early exposure to Joshua 1:8, in which I learned that obedience brings the tangible blessing of God—prosperity and success; a sense of peace, destiny, and relational harmony; an increase in your storehouse.[2] I bought into this in every way, fully engaging this view of God and the implications of this cause-and-effect spiritual world, and yet I had inklings, even early on, that this wasn't quite right.

Enter the India mission trip. During the summer after the healing of my broken ankle, I went on the first of what would be many trips to India. I spent time there helping to build a national youth center and "sharing the gospel" in evangelistic meetings. What was rather obvious was how the learnings of my first year as a Christ-follower didn't seem to compute into Indian culture. The message of discipleship I was exposed to over the last year had an obvious American hue to it. An "obey God and there will be serious reward here and in heaven"[3] message just didn't translate in a culture in which looking for the next meal was the primary focus—not the kind of house you lived in or the amount of money you made. I was only one year into my journey and already enculturated into a specific view of God; and yet I realized that what I was learning didn't preach so well in Punjab, even if it might fly high in Peoria.

India was deeply transformative for other reasons as well. It is the place where I was first exposed to serious human suffering. I remember walking the streets of Bombay (present-day Mumbai) and seeing beggars with the most outrageous deformities imaginable. These were rather common occurrences in Indian culture because of poor nutrition and the lack of prenatal attention and proper medical care. I remember one man whose legs appeared to have been put on backward; I couldn't tell if he was walking backward due to the direction his torso faced or forward due to the direction in which his legs could carry him. I remember seeing a woman with no legs who moved around by using her arms on the ground. I saw a child with two limbs emerging from where arms would be, but the limbs were more like feet than hands and there was no elbow. I saw dead people in the streets and lepers in colonies. I witnessed absolutely bizarre things that I did not have, and still don't have, categories for.

Coming to grips with these kinds of things no doubt has a significant effect on the meaning we find in the experiences of life and on how we understand God. How could I explain what was going on with these things I had seen? In the "good life" Christianity that I had been exposed to, little or no theology of suffering had been developed. What I saw raised questions in my mind, but once everything was out of sight, I could put the human suffering question back on the shelf and let my cause-and-effect view of God remain fully intact and operational for me.

Now I see clearly, and I hope you can too, that we cannot plug in spiritual formulas, such as, "Doing X leads to Y." I used to think so, though I wasn't taught this explicitly. My view of God was implicitly and quietly formed by the teaching I was receiving in the various communities of faith I grew up in. All three of those communities were clearly and sometimes not so carefully molding and forming a worldview, complete with a story or stories about how the world worked, what the end would look like (very soon), and how to plug into God's protection as the end approached. These views of God would have a lasting impact.

Another obvious example of how early experience molds our view of God can be seen in the way in which at our charismatic renewal group (more on that later) we would invite God to be present and not far off. I see clearly now that for all of my childhood and most of my adult years, I have had a spatial view of God. God is out there somewhere, and we invite him here—into our space, into our "area." Of course, at different times I was taught Psalm 139 truth—wherever you go God is already there, for example—but those early experiences took precedence, and as a result, it has taken years to come to a place where my default awareness is of God as present instead of distant.[4]

The view of God as an old man up there somewhere is tough to overcome. None of this teaching was malicious or a denial of God's omnipresence. In fact, one of the things we learn in that hermeneutics class we take when we go away to Bible school or college is that the Bible is full of anthropomorphisms—forms (*morphē*) of God that use human (*anthrōpos*) images to communicate to us.[5] We realize that God isn't only male but has both masculine and feminine attributes; we realize that God isn't embodied out there somewhere but is spirit and everywhere all at once. But early teaching *is* indelible and tough to overcome. Our view of God is quietly molded and shaped. Lenses are softly slipped over our eyes and the frames gently placed on our ears.

Little did I know as a self-assured seventeen-year-old that a new sort of vertigo was just around the corner.

MY THIRD INTERPRETIVE WORLD

My mom had stayed active in the women's Bible study that had prayed for my ankle healing. Between my healed leg, my passion for my high school friends, and my mom's zeal, my dad's interest in spiritual things was piqued. They decided to investigate a new spiritual venue where the whole family could go to grow spiritually. They found a thriving Catholic charismatic prayer group in our community—made up of people my dad knew from his faith tradition who had the power of the Holy Spirit, which my mom was convinced was the key ingredient. Of course, I was fine with this arrangement. Anything that could increase my understanding and excitement about God was a great opportunity as far as I was concerned.

However, instead of answering my questions, the experience raised even deeper ones about how to read the Bible. A dramatic miraculous healing puts someone in the position of easily believing anything they read in the Bible. Miracles, healings, and even "fanciful" things such as talking animals and people who survive in fish for a few days just don't seem crazy—until you have intelligent people you respect start to push back on the very things you have found so easy to understand and believe.

Our new Catholic charismatic group was about to highlight the dramatic differences in the three interpretive worlds I was now a part of: the Presbyterian world of my mom's upbringing, the Italian Catholic world of my father, and the charismatic world we had discovered together.

All three traditions were Christian, to be sure, but that might be about all they shared in common. Each of these worlds brought different perspectives on almost everything—and the differences weren't just about things such as the pope, the role of tradition, and views of Communion. I didn't find those questions particularly interesting or even applicable to my life at that moment. I was more interested in the collision of these three positions on things such as healing and miraculous signs and wonders.

Each tradition had a different take on whether or not prophecy still existed: Was it modern-day preaching? Or was it a spontaneous "word" followed by a "thus saith the Lord." They differed on whether tongues was a heavenly language for devotional praying or simply a missionary aid to help reach people whose language you hadn't learned. Those three worlds had different takes on abortion, homosexuality, and the role of Christ-followers in society and politics. They even differed on how to describe the primary reason Jesus came to earth. No matter what position was voiced, it used the Bible to support it. Each group, each theological position, felt they had biblical footing and a relatively certain corner on the biblical interpretation market.

My Presbyterian pastors—I had three—read the Bible in a particular way: as an inspired historical record of what God did with a particular people in a particular time that we could learn from. The message was quite clear and simple: unequivocal acceptance and love—for pro-choicers and gays, and whoever else needed it. I learned that the church ought to be big on nonjudgmental inclusivism. This position wasn't so appealing to me in my dogmatic high school "I know the Bible" days. My Presby church seemed to be a little loose with the text, in my informed seventeen-year-old interpretive opinion—not taking the Bible very seriously and yet saying all along they really did believe and esteem it.

I remember well the collision of biblical positions. The Catholic charismatic group was going to be present at the Life Chain event, decrying abortion and lining the streets of our town with signs reading "Abortion kills!" The following Sunday in our Presbyterian church, I remember distinctly the pastor telling us that we needed to love those "misguided" fundamentalists who feel a need to picket the streets and attempt to persuade people that a woman shouldn't have a choice in what she can do with her body.

The Catholic take wasn't much different from my Presbyterian experience. We listened to readings every Sunday from the Old Testament, the Gospels, and the Epistles. The interesting thing was that the message (usually referred to as a homily) often didn't connect in any way to the readings for the day—or maybe they did and my high school sensibilities were simply askew.

My experience in Mass after Mass was that the Bible was important, in that we read from it every week, but rather impractical because it didn't get applied to life much. I was undoubtedly less attentive at noon Mass after having survived the 10:30 service at Mom's church; but the reality was that these priests did not connect the Bible to my teenage everyday reality. After a while, I got to the point where I could recite the whole Mass. I knew what the verbal responses were—when to say the creeds, when to lean to the left, lean to the right, stand up, sit down, fight, fight, fight. (Oops, a little Friday night football cheer leaked in there!)

Enter the charismatic renewal meetings we began to attend during my senior year of high school. My Catholic charismatic experience brought intimacy and peace to my formative last year of high school. Here were people who seemed to take the Word of God seriously and at face value. They not only affirmed the miracle of my healing; they really believed the Bible. If it was in the Bible, it was true. If the Bible said something was going to happen, they believed it was going to literally happen. If the Bible says there are talking snakes, then talking snakes there were—and maybe still could be. If Jesus could heal blind people and paralytics too, then he still can and will.

They believed the Bible all right. They believed *everything* in the Bible and expected everything it said to still be happening today. Why? Because the Bible says that "Jesus Christ is the same yesterday and today and forever" (Hebrews 13:8), so what he did then he will do again for you right now. They believed the Bible in a new kind of way. They believed stuff I had never considered believing. For these people, God is present, immediate, and always wanting to speak to us and tell us things.

This view of the Spirit of God solves a lot of interpretation problems for the people in the movement because if you don't understand something in the Bible, you pray and ask the Holy Spirit to show you. Interpretation was moved from the realm of mind to the realm of spirit, from the intellect to the soul. You'd think this move from head to heart might have tempered the certainty factor; but it didn't. When the Holy Spirit speaks, it is so personal, so intimate, so unmistakable that the certainty question is even more deeply entrenched. We can be certain of what the Holy Spirit tells us precisely because it bypasses the faulty and unreliable intellect. The intellect cannot really know the things of God apart from the Spirit, so why engage the middleman? This was the conclusion taught numerous times in this group. Their favorite passage for this idea was 1 Corinthians 2.

Other than my Sunday morning experiences, which weren't big on Bible teaching, this was my first exposure to real biblical instruction. The only companions in my interpretive journey thus far had been authors I had been reading during the past year; but much of what I heard with this group seemed to confirm my developing understanding.

THE HAUNTINGS

We all have to fight against a tendency toward selective listening that hunts for material to buttress our certainty scale. Certainty seems to often lurk in the background of our minds as a premium value to carry with us throughout our Christian experience. I was about to get my first dose of just how deeply entrenched certainty is when I had the opportunity to hear someone else give their take on the "master verse" of 2 Timothy 3:16–17.

There were four or five men who shared the responsibility of teaching in the charismatic prayer group, and it was Bill's turn on this particular Sunday night. *Inspired by God* was the phrase getting attention. We were told that the word *inspired* literally means "breathed by God." Bill built a persuasive case that these words spoken by God were forever the truth and therefore without any errors, making the Bible a fixed record of God's rules to be obeyed. These rules were set in stone; they were mandates for life. A lot of books out there would seek our attention, Bill told us. A lot of people would claim authority. But only one book has authority — and that is this one called the Bible, because it is the only one inspired by God. All of this made total and complete sense to me. But two unsettling things would gnaw at and haunt me for years.

Haunting Rumination #1

My first haunting rumination resulted from the English literature class I was taking in high school. We were reading Shakespeare. I wasn't a fan of Shakespeare. I found his works boring and hard to understand — and still don't like them much. (I know, I'm uncultured.) Bill's teaching on 2 Timothy 3 came at the end of the same week my teacher in English Lit had talked about the power of classic texts to mold people's lives, even to mold whole cultures and societies.

I don't think anything would have been problematic if my teacher hadn't used the word *inspired* in class. Several times Mrs. M referred to Shakespeare as "inspired" and other English literature poets and authors as "inspiring." (By the way, Mrs. M is what we really called her. I thought she was old then and recently found out she had just died. How is it that those you thought were ancient when you were in high school live for many more decades?) Mrs.

M never made a biblical connection or took on a biblical view of inspiration; but her repetitive use that week of the word around non-Christian literature ended up being a point of intrigue for me as I sat at Sunday night's teaching with Bill.

The Bible was inspired. Was Shakespeare inspired? If so, by whom? The literature gods? Is there a connection? And what about this idea of classics molding lives? We had had a few conversations about how classics become classics—an organic process that over generations eventually "canonizes" this literature as great and worthy of being passed on. So how does a classic exert its influence? Does it matter? Is it connected to how the Bible exerts influence? I had no answers for these questions, but they were brought into sharp focus that week. I put them on the back shelf of my mind.

The one big thing I noticed, however, was how dramatically different Bill and Mrs. M's understandings of inspiration were—in fact, polar opposites. Bill taught that God's inspiring the text meant he gave us a set of errorless, timeless truths. Inspiration for Bill solidified, codified, concretized, and freeze-framed the Bible forevermore—Amen. The role of the disciple was to mine those truths and apply them. Applying those truths and living by them was the only way to blessing, and to do so even ensured blessing. When you live God's Word, he *has* to bless you. Something in me could resonate with that. I had memorized Joshua 1:6–9, after all, and that passage promised success in whatever I did.

Inspired to Mrs. M meant "dynamic; enlivened; a living, creeping power; a pulsating-with-life document that had the ability to get on the inside of you and quietly work you over, tweaking your heart and thoughts." Far from the static, mechanical, stiffening view of inspiration that encased God's Word in stone, Mrs. M talked of classics being "inhabited by power." She spoke of unruly narratives that captured imaginations, of passages of wonder that connected us to visceral and primal urges. Mrs. M's description sounded so alive to me, and Bill's sounded so dead.

Something felt strange in all that. Shouldn't Mrs. M's description apply more to the Bible than to any other book on the planet? If so, what about Bill's understanding? But were these simply their own understandings of inspiration filtered through their unique abilities to communicate? Or was there something here I was to learn? This question lives on in me today.

Haunting Rumination #2

The second issue I struggled with was a bit more complex. This, too, was brought into sharp relief by Bill's teaching that night.

In Study some months earlier, we had had what was a rather disquieting conversation about 2 Timothy 3. We were trying to figure out which "Scripture" Paul was referring to when he said to Timothy that "all Scripture is God-breathed." Now, on the surface this seems easy to answer: *all of it*. The whole Bible is "all Scripture." Not a satisfactory answer, though, for our resident National Merit scholar Dean, known for his probing questions and thoughtful articulation. He raised a concern that when Paul wrote his letter to Timothy, the Scripture he was referring to couldn't have been the Bible in our hands that night because it didn't even exist at the time of Paul's writing. Dean pointed out Paul didn't know that the letter he was writing to Timothy would someday be included in the Bible. In other words, the New Testament as we were studying it that night wasn't even in existence when Paul was writing to Timothy—which was true of *every letter* Paul wrote. None of those letters were at the time of their writing "Scripture." If this is true, Dean reasoned, then which "Scripture" is 2 Timothy 3 pointing to?

Dean posed a comparative illustration to help us in the group understand what he was driving at. He was very good at that sort of thing. He suggested that if he were to write a letter to me and state verbatim 2 Timothy 3:6–17, he wouldn't expect his letter in which these words were written to be included in the phrase "all Scripture." He was simply writing a letter to me to affirm a truth he believed about all Scripture. He could also write a dozen personal letters to everyone in the room and certainly wouldn't expect that his statements made to me in my personal letter about "all Scripture" would apply in any way to the other personal letters he wrote to the others in the room. So, he posed, why do we think 2 Timothy 3 applies to the New Testament? What makes us think 2 Timothy 3 applies to the other letters Paul wrote? Sharp and insightful Dean raised a question none of us could answer or even fully understand.

This was the conversation swirling around when Bill decided to teach on 2 Timothy 3. Bill's teaching that night railroaded right through the question as though it didn't even exist. He said it was clear that this passage applies to the whole Bible, and "if it doesn't apply to the whole Bible in my hands tonight, then it doesn't apply to any of it." I heard his point and part of me agreed, but part of me wanted to raise my hand and ask the hard question that Dean had raised. I didn't. The question, however, lived on, just as my first gnawing question did.

BASIC INSTRUCTIONS BEFORE LEAVING EARTH

Learning the View of God and Eschatology

ARE THERE MORE riveting movies than those that depict the end of the world? We have a fascination with *how* it will happen, *why* it will happen, and *when* it will happen. When this fascination intersects certain brands of biblical interpretation, we are in for some novel ways of handling Scripture, some very interesting possible end-time plot projections, and an overall aura of fear and urgency. The charismatic group I was involved with was all in on all of the above. These were the days of Hal Lindsey, the precursor to Tim LaHaye of Left Behind fame. While Lindsay's material (think *The Late Great Planet Earth*) wasn't written in the form of a novel, his theological disposition was from the same cloth as that of LaHaye: you must read the Bible literally and you have to realize the end-time stuff talked about in the Gospels (see Matthew 24 and Mark 13) is yet to come. And so we have the opportunity to read each day's newspaper headlines in light of the Gospels and determine beyond a shadow of a doubt whether we are in the "end times" and whether Jesus will be returning in our generation.

INSIGHTFUL HEADLINES ...?

I came to realize much later in my schooling that this study of the end times was called *eschatology* and that it exerts influence over almost every other thing in terms of how people read and appropriate the Bible. The Presbyterian Church never once talked about the end of the world or the passages in the Bible that spoke about it; nor did any of my Catholic experiences tune me in to these biblical tones.

But the charismatic renewal group? Wow! You didn't have to be there for many weeks before you would hear prophecy, usually from one of two women, that the end was near and we needed to be prepared and Jesus was coming to take those who were holy and ready. They genuinely believed that Jesus was returning in their lifetime and that it was our singular job to prepare ourselves. When you have a framing story that the end is near and that Jesus' return is just around the corner, it informs your urgency — your behavior, your expectancy, and undoubtedly your evangelistic zeal.

Bill and Jim, two of the teachers, would regularly teach from the end-times passages. Their urgency would lead them to use some fairly scary tactics to help people get their lives squared away — a lot of fear, pleadings about our urgent need to go out and win the world because the Bible was crystal clear, reminders that the end was just a few headlines away. But was it? Bill and Jim were fond of reciting what I discovered was an old vacation Bible school saying — one I hadn't heard. The Bible essentially contains Basic Instructions Before Leaving Earth. The acronym was a way of remembering the essential reason we were given the Bible.

At some level, this wasn't foreign to me. In Study we often con-cluded that the Bible was full of instructions on how to live. But what we hadn't connected until the emergence of the Hal Lindsey material was how the instructions in the Bible were given, or, I should say, supposedly given, for the express purpose of the "exit planet Earth" scenario. The point of life was to prepare to leave life on the planet. Reading the Bible was to be informed by an ever-present threat/blessing that the end of the universe was near.

These are conversations I would take back to Study for mulling around with my teenage friends. In fact, some of them came with me a few times to sample the hoopla I was experiencing. As time went on, though, the view and study of Scripture being expressed in that meeting had substantial disconnects with what we had been embarking on for the last number of months in Study. We were having honest conversations about such passages as Matthew 24. Dean, of course, had probing questions—questions such as, If the disciples were asking a question of Jesus in the third verse of Matthew 24 and the response Jesus gave referred to events still two thousand-plus years away, how was it that Jesus was answering the question? How was his answer in any way applicable to the dis-ciples? In our thinking and language in Study, what was for "them back there" and what was for us right now?

Dean happened to be taking a high school class called Mythol-ogy. The teacher was deeply engaged in a local church and saw many parallels between biblical stories and mythology in general. Dean would ask him questions and then bring the issues to Study for further dialogue. Dean's teacher, Mr. Vandercook, concluded that the fact that Matthew 24 is literally going to be fulfilled some two thousand-plus years after Matthew wrote it isn't the only way the passage can be read—and in fact isn't the most common way it has been understood throughout church history. There were a few other options — options that didn't appear in *The Late Great Planet Earth* or in the teaching I was getting on Sunday nights. How were we to choose between them? And were there other ones we simply didn't know about?

Those of us in Study couldn't pull all of our questions and answers together into a cohesive whole; but we could see that disconnections existed among various views and that a growing number of views undermined our "certainty" value. We fumbled around, discussed, and dissected things from every angle seventeen-year-olds can invent; but we didn't have any blinding insights that would reconcile our B.I.B.L.E. view with the view we heard from Mr. Vandercook, namely, that most of the material in Matthew 24 had already been fulfilled in the lifetime of the disciples.

WE ALL WEAR LENSES FOR READING

The critical learning for me and for others in Study was how our view of the Bible was dramatically influenced by our view of God. If we believed that God was orchestrating an end-of-the-world scenario, then we would hold a different view of why the Bible is given to us from the view that God is getting us to connect with him so we can live in some idealized way to receive his blessing. Those were the two options on our table of conversation at the moment, but we all felt there must be others. Those others were forthcoming, but they would have to wait until I embarked on my first formal upper-level schooling experience.

There you have it — the formative years that set the trajectory of my spiritual journey, interest in the Bible, and even the approach to and questions I have about the Bible. These molding influences set the course — not an unalterable course, but a course nonetheless. The subsequent years in an undergraduate school, a master's program, and a doctoral program were also molding experiences but in different ways. By the time I made it to those steps in my development, much was already established. We inherit and adopt views of the Bible that remain largely blind-spot assumptions. Those assumptions are learned and assimilated long before we have any apparatus available to determine if the assumptions are good, bad, or outright misleading. As a result of our exposure to a Christian community, we are taught a view of the Bible held by that community, and it is assumed that this approach is true. We therefore adopt it too. We usually don't go investigating these approaches, questioning them, or looking for alternative possibilities because at this stage we don't even know that alternatives exist.

Once a viewpoint is in place and an approach to Scripture adopted, we have a default setting to evaluate what we hear. But giving in to our default is exactly what prevents us from reading the Bible in new and fresh ways.

When I was going to our charismatic renewal group and hearing all the passages about the end times, our teachers repeatedly said, "Don't just believe what we tell you; go and look at these passages yourself." That all sounds very noble, but often when you have been given a certain set of glasses to look through as you read the text, then being encouraged to read the Bible and investigate "all this for yourself" will do nothing but affirm what they have told you. Why? Because *the lenses determine what you see.*

When a teacher presents an interpretation of Matthew 24 that argues that none of these things have literally happened yet — the sun hasn't turned dark and the moon hasn't ceased giving light and stars haven't fallen from the sky (see verse 29) — and must yet be fulfilled, this sort of reasoning sounds compelling. Wearing those lenses won't allow you to see any other options for the text. The question doesn't really lie with the text; it lies with the way in which we approach the text. Therefore, investigating these passages on your own to verify how truthful the teacher has or hasn't been in their teaching is to merely affirm in your reading what they have already taught you to see. In other words, you will conclude they are right. You checked them out, and the text says exactly what they told you it said.

We need to rid ourselves of these blind-spot assumptions.

I'm not saying we can study without lenses of some sort. We all have them. But what we often don't realize is that we *do* have them. I meet people nearly every day of the week who are convinced that they wear no lenses whatsoever and are objectively reading the Bible with *the* correct interpretation. We inherit glasses in such subtle ways that we often don't even know we have a set.

When we begin reading the Bible, we usually do so because we want to investigate God, or we have come to follow Jesus and know the Bible is the manual to help us get in touch with that new relationship. The community of faith we enter will provide a set of lenses for viewing the text. And those lenses come to us in the midst of new discovery, excitement, and investigation. We are hardly sitting around asking questions such as, "Is this the right approach to the Bible? What other lenses can I choose to use?"

As a teenager, I didn't realize I was inheriting my first set of lenses. But after being in the ministry for over thirty years, I have found this issue to be no respecter of age. Almost all new Bible readers I have encountered in the last three decades have an inherited set of lenses—assumptions—and are relatively convinced they are the right ones. The formative teachings and experiences they have had are no different from mine. Our inherited approaches to the Bible stick. They stick, then become ingrained and entrenched, and sometimes are held on to with fundamentalist zeal. While many things may be unclear to us, we *are* certain of our view of the Bible, and we don't want anybody to mess with it!

PART 2

MY THEOLOGICAL JOURNEY

Reading the Script with Fresh Eyes

My theological journey started in earnest in my biblical schooling both in undergraduate and graduate school. The questions raised early on in my high school years about how to approach the Bible — well, I thought these would be answered in a more academic context. New methods were acquired, new tools were employed, and new spiritual practices and relationships were enjoyed. These "new" things were taken into pastoral ministry, where I passed on the knowledge I had gained.

But throughout my academic and pastoral journey the questions I had always asked about the approach to the text and about the lenses through which we see remained largely unanswered. In fact, I had a growing sense of dissatisfaction with the pick-and-choose method of application I had been taught. I wasn't disenchanted with God or the church but simply unsatisfied with how the Bible was being used.

And I wasn't alone.

The questions I had were the very questions people in the church I served were asking. I didn't have answers. There were no easy ways to deal with such issues as Abraham's hearing God tell him to sacrifice his son, or Solomon's having hundreds of wives and concubines, or women being silent in the church. In the midst of the fresh discoveries in the Scriptures nourishing my life, there were still unsolvables, and difficult unsolvables — and to make matters worse, the list was growing and becoming so large that these questions just couldn't be ignored.

I knew for some time that I had inherited lenses; the big discovery now was the *type* of lenses I was wearing. For the first time, I took them off and really inspected them to see if they were serving me well. I also picked up some new glasses and tried them on. Part 2 is an effort to sketch the contours of that journey — a journey more and more people are on or are desiring to take.

SELECTIVE APPLICATION

Silencing Women and Selling All You Have

THE OPPORTUNITY TO study the Bible in several academic settings with brilliant men and women has been a great gift to me and one of my most cherished life experiences. When you enter seminary to do master's or doctoral work, you find that there are "standard" conversations all new students want to engage in—matters dealing with these kinds of questions:

- Does the Bible support the idea that everything has been preplanned and predetermined, or do we have free will?
- Are the original documents of the Bible written perfectly and without error (documents we don't have, so we have no way of proving it), or is the Bible simply reliable in matters of faith and life?
- Were John Calvin and Martin Luther theologically more accurate, or were the popes and the Catholic church more on target?

Guys and gals who attend these learning institutions typically have a high interest in these questions, and there is a relatively predictable pattern to how these issues (and a host of others) will be sorted out during the years of theological training.

The summary statement, however, of what a person is trying to learn during their education is *how to study the Bible* to accurately understand its message and to communicate its truth so Christ-followers can experience life change and those not yet in the family of God can find Jesus. All the theology classes, all the language classes, all the pastoral counseling classes have this overarching purpose.

My time in school highlighted the very issues and questions I wanted to resolve. How do we know what was for "them back there" and how do we know what was meant to apply to us. Same old questions, different context. Can I wear fabric with mixed fibers while being forbidden from getting a tattoo? I know we aren't doing the concubine thing anymore (Solomon surely had a bunch!), but what about women braiding their hair? Is that still forbidden (see 1 Timothy 2:9)?

Let me share some concrete examples to illustrate the magnitude of this issue of how we approach the Bible and how many of these issues remained almost entirely unresolved for me. I want to focus on some well-known passages so we can come to grips with just how much our lenses/assumptions inform our reading and application.

THE HOT ONE

As I went into my master's program, I walked right into the hotbed of controversy concerning the women in ministry issue. In my seminary, vocal advocates stood on both sides of the question. Some of these men were immersed in the fray, writing some of the articles helping to shape the national conversation.[1] While the women-in-ministry question might be one of the most volatile in recent years, it certainly isn't the only one. Still, it shows how the questions we ask and the lenses we wear will yield a particular kind of result.

Paul's words to Timothy serve as the passage in question:

> I also want women to dress modestly, with decency and propriety, not with braided hair or gold or pearls or expensive clothes, but with good deeds, appropriate for women who profess to worship God.
>
> A woman should learn in quietness and full submission. I do not permit a woman to teach or to have authority over a man; she must be silent. For Adam was formed first, then Eve. And Adam was not the one deceived; it was the woman who was deceived and became a sinner. But women will be saved through childbearing—if they continue in faith, love and holiness with propriety.
>
> 1 TIMOTHY 2:9–15 NIV

There are multiple issues in the debate, but the one most germane for our conversation is how you pick and choose. If verse 12 is in effect—women cannot teach men and must be silent—then aren't they also forbidden to braid their hair and wear gold or pearls (verse 9)? How do you determine which verses are for them back there and which are for all time? Believe me, I know the technical arguments on both sides of the question, but I am afraid that all the technical explanations do not even begin to do justice to the simplicity of the question.

The issue this passage raises is the same one we will constantly run into. How do we pick and choose? Why one verse and not another? The conundrums are thorny and intractable, and they force us to do gymnastics with the text. And what about those who have had no technical training? If those with all the language skills, exegetical tools, and degrees can't figure it out, what about the average gal sitting in church on Sunday who is being encouraged to read her Bible each day? What is she to do?

NOAH AND NIC

Most of us are quite familiar with the story of Noah. At a key juncture in the history of humanity's emergence onto the world scene, God decides to call a do-over and enters a conversation with Noah. He gives Noah the brief rundown and historical sketch of the problem: Humans have flubbed things pretty good. God is not only disappointed but is having second thoughts about this whole creation thing. With a little reflection, though, he has decided that he would like to enter a partnership with Noah and asks for some buy-in. Noah can see God's point and even shares his concerns, so he asks for details. "Simple," God says, and he hands him elaborate and detailed blueprints for building a mammoth yacht — highly unusual since there's no rain in the forecast. But knowing it is best not to question God, Noah heads down to his local 84 Lumber store and starts buying.

When we read the Noah story in Genesis, we can extract many lessons and "morals of the story." We can make countless conclusions about just how the Noah story applies to us. In your experience you have probably heard more than one possibility as to the impact this story should have on our lives. A few quick examples will suffice.

We find out in Genesis 6:9 that Noah was one who walked with God and was blameless. We might conclude we are about to read an example of what it looks like to walk with God and live a blameless life. We might conclude that the Noah narrative is about how to exercise faith when God tells you to do something outlandish (such as build a boat the size of a football field). We might see Noah as a new Adam figure, starting over in the world and receiving the same mandate given to Adam and Eve about being fruitful and multiplying. We might point to one of several applications, or to all of them, as the point of the story.

It's interesting to note before we go further that we are *assuming* there is some application, some moral of the story, we are supposed to be capturing. I know of no one who has ever suggested there is no application from the Noah story, that it is simply some historical material that sketches how God is interacting with his creation. I will come back to this a little later and investigate where these assumptions about whether there is supposed to be application come from.

While there are all sorts of conclusions we may make about the main point of the story — or we may have many takeaways — what I have never heard preached (and my guess is you haven't either) is that you and I are being instructed in this Genesis story to go and build a boat just like Noah's. I don't think I have ever heard of anyone making a big lumber purchase and undertaking a boat-building project to those specifications in their front yard. I have never heard of a preacher or teacher trying to persuade their hearers that the main application is building a large boat for an extended camping trip, complete with wildlife aboard. Of course, we all think this is a bit preposterous and certainly not the point of the story, at least for us. We would readily conclude that this boat-building scheme was only for "them back there" and that there is probably something else we are to take away and apply.

Let's hold that thought and proceed to another story.

One day Jesus is unwinding from a hard day of ministry meetings and hands-on training sessions with the disciples, when he hears a knock at the door. He doesn't recognize the fella, who introduces himself as Nic and asks if he can have a quick word with

Jesus. Jesus invites him in, and Nic proceeds with a quick introductory background so Jesus has some framework for Nic's observations. Of course, all Nic had to say was that he was a Pharisee, and Jesus pretty much had all the info he needed. Nic proceeds to share with Jesus that while he knows that the Pharisees really don't like Jesus' liberal approach to Sabbath, food, and circumcision laws—and as a result think the works Jesus is doing are from the Devil—Nic wants to register a different spin from that of his colleagues.

Nicodemus makes an observation: "These works you are doing, Jesus, contrary to the opinion of my colleagues, point in my mind to the fact that you are from God." It was a simple comment, a courageous claim, and a huge departure from public Pharisee opinion. Jesus responds in essence, "Nic, for you to see this stuff as the manifestation of the kingdom [the word used in John 3:3 is *see*] and not that of the Enemy is truly a point of departure. This sort of seeing only happens when you are undergoing a paradigm shift—a being born again, a radical rethinking, a genuine re-viewing of the situation. Seeing my work as kingdom work is big stuff. And if you want to enter into that type of kingdom, it happens only as you yield and respond to the unpredictably directioned Spirit, who blows like the wind. You can't see it, but you surely can feel it."

I am reading John 3 a bit differently from the typical evangelical reading. The reading of most evangelicals replaces the word *see* in verse 3 with *enter* and swaps the words *kingdom of God* in verse 3 for *heaven, the place you go when you die.* As a result, this verse has become a litmus test for many with regard to whether or not you are going to heaven when you die.

Here is our interpretive dilemma, and it is no small thing: Why does God's talking to Noah and commanding him to do something like build a boat not apply to us when Jesus' act of talking to Nicodemus and his message about being born again does? Both passages tell of God's talking to good guys whose names start with N. In the Noah story, God commands something; in the Nic story, Jesus commends Nic for his willingness to depart from his colleagues' party line. Why is one assumed to apply to us and the other isn't? Why is applying the application of the Noah story confined to secondary details of the story when the real faith exhibited was building a boat of that magnitude while those around him had to be thinking he was nuts; yet when we come to a Pharisee named Nicodemus, we rewrite the story to make it sound as though he was asking a question about how to get into the afterlife (which is clearly not the case)—and then by swapping a few words, we have what has become an evangelical litmus test for believing the Bible literally. Ironically, given the watershed passage John 3 has become, it is the only place where the topic of "being born again" is discussed. Peter speaks of being "born again" of imperishable seed (1 Peter 1:23), but this is the closest we get to this single story about Nicodemus.

My point is this: Our picking and choosing as to what applies, how it applies, and how important it is doesn't always have a lot of thought and reflection behind it. As I travel and talk to people about the Bible, I find that this picking and choosing is leaving the average Bible reader in a less than confident position about what applies and how to apply it. Many of these interpretive challenges exist. And let me be clear here: I have no desire to undermine anyone's faith—in fact, quite the opposite. I'm hoping that as we unravel the snags that confuse us, we would be able to come up with better ways of handling the biblical text and ultimately possess an even richer, deeper faith. If all we had to unravel were one or two stories, it'd be one thing—but this isn't the case. Let's look at a couple more examples.

SELLING ALL YOU HAVE, REALLY?

Unlike the Nicodemus narrative, the story of the wealthy Yuppie (Luke 18:18–30), as it is often called—uh, sorry, it's usually called "the parable of the rich young ruler"—is about how to gain eternal life. When the young Bentley-driving, Fortune 500 executive asks Jesus what he must do to inherit eternal life, Jesus responds with a very interesting answer: obey the commands. Now without going any further, are we cool with that answer? I mean cool to the point we would preach it? Or have we figured out a way around the plain words of this text?

What is the problem you ask? The answer Jesus gave is precisely what we would typically label as *law*, not *grace*. The standard Bible answer is that you cannot do *anything* to inherit eternal life; it is only by grace through faith, not by works, says Paul in Ephesians 2:8–9. But that's not what Jesus said.

Bentley Boy, after asking Jesus which commands he needs to keep, nonchalantly responds by saying he is already keeping those and asks *what else* he should do. Jesus raises the bar and gives the punch line: "Sell everything you have.... Then come, follow me" (Luke 18:22). Our young exec walks away dejected and defeated because he had a big portfolio, and selling everything was simply not in the cards.

So what's the point of the story? What is the takeaway? Surely we haven't told people to obey all the rules so they can go to heaven, and my guess is we probably won't do so anytime soon—and yet this is one of the very few passages where Jesus has a conversation about entering the afterlife.

Compare how we apply (or don't apply) this passage with how we muscle the John 3 Nicodemus story into saying stuff it doesn't say. Notice the way we change one passage to make it a litmus test for "getting in" and summarily dismiss the other passage that directly addresses "getting in." What is going on with how we use the text of the Bible?

I have heard some people say the Noah story doesn't apply because it is in the Old Testament, but the Nic story does because it is in the New. But if simply being part of the New Testament determines whether a passage is applicable, we're left wondering how we are supposed to apply the rich young ruler material of Luke 18.[2]

ONLY FOUR THINGS, NOT FIVE?

For the last several decades, we have had waves of conversation about what it means to be a New Testament church (sometimes called an "Acts 2 church"). I will be the first to say this is all well-intentioned, noble, appropriate, and right-headed to a degree. So let's look briefly at Acts 2, where we have another story with similar tones (or at least a similar note) to the parable of the rich young ruler.

Each fall, my church (like many churches) launches our small group ministry. There is no lack of small group resources and curriculum to help churches see their groups flourish and succeed. One of the nearly universal common denominators in these launches, resources, and curriculums is the quoting of Acts 2:42–47 as support for why we need to do small groups.

Before we look at these verses, let's ask a question: Do we need to use biblical passages as support to launch small groups? Do we really need biblical support to do the things we do in the church? Oh, I know the knee-jerk answer: Of course we do! But really? We only have to see a few examples to realize that most of what we do on any given Sunday is extrabiblical—not found in the Bible or not forbidden by it. Some people are beginning to see that citing verses to "prove" why we need to do this or that is actually causing us more trouble than it is clarifying why we are doing what we are doing.

Now let's consider these verses from Acts 2:

> They [members of the early church] devoted themselves to the apostles' teaching and to fellowship, to the breaking of bread and to prayer. Everyone was filled with awe at the many wonders and signs performed by the apostles. All the believers were together and had everything in common. They sold property and possessions to give to anyone who had need. Every day they continued to meet together in the temple courts. They broke bread in their homes and ate together with glad and sincere hearts, praising God and enjoying the favor of all the people. And the Lord added to their number daily those who were being saved.
>
> ACTS 2:42–47

Commonly the first four items above (teaching, fellowship, breaking of bread, prayer) are cited, expounded on, taught, and elevated as part of the biblical model for how we need to do community together and hence be an "Acts 2 church." Of course, we are quick to desire the blessing of the Acts 2 church: "The Lord added to their number daily."

So here is my question: Why are the first four items elevated as the magical combination for being the New Testament church and not the verses 44 and 45 part of selling property and possessions and holding it in common with the rest of the people in your church or small group? Certainly this is no more or less important to the Acts 2 church than teaching, socializing, eating, and praying. Or what about the fact that they met together *daily* (verse 46). Should this be a requirement to be a New Testament Acts 2 church?

These are not nitpicky questions. They go to the very heart of how we are interpreting and then applying Scripture to our lives. If we can so universally model our small group ministries on this passage—and let me say again, with noble and God honoring intentions—but be selective in applying it, aren't we back to the same old pick-and-choose problem that launched us into this conversation?

How have we managed to apply part of this passage and not the other part? Many have tended to say that the things mentioned in these latter verses are simply cultural and therefore not applicable to us, just for "them back there." Fair enough, and all good by me, but just what criteria are we using for determining what is simply cultural and no longer applicable. Might it not be argued that, with our consumerist American culture—and even the church at times seeming to have been hijacked by consumerism—a rigorous application of "surrendering our possessions" is in order? Could doing so make a huge statement to the rest of the world?

I'm toying with our thinking a bit here. I am not arguing for a new Christian socialism, Marxism, or Communism. However, by pointing to several well-known and frequently used passages, I'm showing that our approach to applying the Bible is riddled with inconsistencies that become increasingly painful as we seek to explain to an inquisitive world why we believe what we believe and why we act or don't act the way we do.

The problem we encounter isn't related merely to communicating with the world. Those of us in the church have trouble clearly explaining to each other how we randomly select what is in force for us today and what is for "them back there."

THE GUIDING QUESTION CRYSTALLIZED

Uncovering the Dominant Hermeneutic

WHEN YOU HEAD to an undergraduate school to do work in biblical studies, one of the classes you take early on is called *hermeneutics*—a fancy mouthful of a word for "the principles of Bible study." As you progress in school, you take increasingly complex levels of this discipline to equip you to study the Bible and to help others learn to study the Bible too.

As I walked into my advanced hermeneutics class during the second year of my master's program, an interesting discussion ensued that would continue to clarify and draw out the application issues I had already been struggling with for about eight years. We were having a conversation about Acts 10. You may remember that this story is about how, in God's economy, Gentiles—those who were not Jewish (Cornelius and family)—were also being included in the family of God. Gentile inclusion wasn't the focus of our troubling seminary class conversation, though; the narrative about Peter was the disruptive flash point.

One day Peter is out on his roof for a time of centering prayer while he waits for the noonday meal to be prepared. The text tells us he is hungry, an important detail in light of what is about to happen (Acts 10:10). While waiting and praying he falls into a trance — a fact notable in my mind simply because in the charismatic renewal group I had previously attended, trances were considered demonic and anathema.

Back to the story. In the trance, Peter sees a knapsack dropped from heaven that is full of all sorts of creatures — edible stuff, but stuff written off the menu of any Jew who keeps dietary laws and a kosher kitchen (see Leviticus 11). The Spirit of God issues a command: "Get up, Peter. Kill and eat" (Acts 10:13). Peter refuses, saying he would surely not eat any of those creatures because they were unclean and he had never eaten anything unclean. This scene repeats itself — and the voice speaks a second time: "Do not call anything impure that God has made clean" (verse 15). And then the scene repeats a third time. When the trance is over, Peter tries to figure out the meaning of what has just happened.

God was preparing Peter for an event about to unfold. Cornelius, an unclean, impure Gentile, is going to serve as an object lesson for Peter to show that even the impure Gentiles are being included in God's story. Peter's trance was used to illustrate the *inclusion* of Cornelius.

The story seems straightforward enough, the main point relatively obvious. But in class someone raised a question that baffled even my "PhD from Cambridge" professor. Mike asked, "Would we as future pastors be OK with someone coming to us and saying that in a dream/vision/trance God had told them to do something clearly contradictory to his written word? As a model of illumination, as a testimony to the Holy Spirit's leading, would we be OK with that?"

Mike's question brought silence to the room. The underlying assumption he was making was fairly common—namely, that the Spirit of God would never tell you to do something contradictory to God's written Word—but this assumption seemed to fall apart as we read Acts 10. Mike was driving at a core issue: Do we subscribe to ideas and principles that apply to *us* in some mysterious way but not to the very *biblical characters* we are reading about?

Why would we create a principle, "God would never give you any subjective leading that is out of sync or contradictory with what is revealed in his written word"—a principle commonly repeated in pulpits and even in seminary classrooms—that so obviously isn't found or modeled in the very text we are studying? A tough question to be sure, one for which there is no easy answer.

Peter's situation wasn't the only one. How do we feel about Abraham, for example? Let's say a respected elder in the church you attend pulls you aside and confides that God is really testing his faith. God has told him to take his son on an overnight camp-out and kill the boy at the campfire. His rationale? Abraham and Isaac in Genesis 22. I don't know of anyone who has read the text of Genesis 22 and made that conclusion, but how do we square what Abraham heard from God when we know that killing is just plain wrong?

FILLING A PRESCRIPTION OR GETTING A DESCRIPTION

My professor's explanation of the Acts 10 passage was a nice attempt to sound academic, but he totally skirted the hard issue. His response is one often made about content in the book of Acts: Since Acts is primarily a history book about the birth of the church—a transitional and unique era—we have to be careful to distinguish between what is descriptive and prescriptive, what is to be applied and what represents backstory.

A bit of translation is helpful here. *Descriptive* material describes events and situations. Clearly Peter's trance and interaction with the Spirit is being described. *Prescriptive* material gives us directions or prescriptions for behavior. My professor's explanation of the material in Acts 10? Peter's narrative was descriptive, not prescriptive.

But nobody bought that. And here is why.

First, most of the New Testament is about a transitional and unique era. If we adopt this line of reasoning, we cannot have anything in the Gospels apply in any meaningful way. Second, we don't live consistently with this distinction. What do we do, for example, with the Acts 2:42–47 passage we use to support our desire to build our small group ministries? This passage surely isn't prescriptive; it is merely a description of what the early church did. Nowhere does it say these are the most important, long-term, and abiding elements that every church for all time and in all places needs to mimic.

So back to the Peter narrative of Acts 10. Nothing in the text is prescriptive, just descriptive. So does nothing apply? Is it simply a historical narrative giving us important background on the roots of the church and how it was founded?

These are not mere rhetorical questions. They get at a real issue that needs to be more carefully explored as we dive in further.

The reason I introduced the distinction between prescription and description is because there is a good chance you'll encounter this line of reasoning. That which is simply described has no force for us today; it is for "them back there." But material that is prescribed is stuff we need to build our lives around.

The problem, of course, is there are many places in which the distinction doesn't hold up. We create principles that when applied simply don't work. It isn't enough for those in the academy to say there are always exceptions to the rules because they aren't even clear on the exceptions; and if *they* aren't, how will the average person like you and me recognize and evaluate the exceptions?

I realize this may seem to be just a dry and dusty academic exercise, but it represents exactly the kind of things people asked me about every week of my twenty years in pastoral ministry. Justin, an elder in a church in Georgia, told me recently, "Ron, my spiritual growth coach gave me a verse that is very important to him, and he thinks it applies to my situation. But it's a line spoken by a prophet to the people of Israel. Can it really be used as a lever to get me to do something? Does this really apply to me? And is this the way we're supposed to be applying the Bible?"

This is far from academic irrelevancy. When people read the Bible, they are trying to discern *how they are to live.* They don't know if having a dream like Peter's is a legitimate thing. They don't know if they have to stop wearing jewelry, as Paul suggests in 1 Timothy 2:9.

In my academic course work, I came across all sorts of hermeneutical theories—fancy complicated models to engage the text. We spoke of recovering or uncovering the author's intention in what he wrote and of what the text meant then and what it means or how it applies today. We talked about cultural background; sociological context; linguistic theory; first-century origins, manners, and customs surrounding the biblical characters; and narrative patterns. All of these theories in some way or another were developed to help us get at the real meaning of the text.

All of the theories had one thing in common: they sought to answer the grand question, "What is irrelevant for application today, and what is to be obeyed today?" Many of these theories seem on the surface to complicate more than clarify. But in the end, I really do think they have a desire to try to come to grips with what the text says so we can eventually be shaped by it.

If the Bible is a book given to us by God, shouldn't it be relatively accessible? Not simple, but accessible. Shakespeare's writings are challenging; it takes work to understand them, but his body of work is accessible if you put in the effort. If we can't even agree at the academic level how to get at the text, do we just throw our hands in the air and give up? If scholars engage in heated, endless debates about straightforward passages in an attempt to determine what is cultural and what isn't, then what are *we* supposed to do?

WHY IS THIS THE QUESTION?

Surely agnosticism about our approach to the Bible isn't the solution. Throwing our hands in the air isn't the solution either. We have to explore other possibilities. The issue is pressing and isn't going away. People have questions about how to interpret and use the Bible.

People ask me how a tithing passage (Malachi 3:6–12) can have any relevance to forcing/mandating people to tithe today. People ask me about the homosexual issue, wanting to know if it really was the same issue in Paul's day and how it applies now. All of the questions stem from one set of lenses being worn that causes us to ask one big question: If the Bible is the owner's manual for life, if it is Basic Instructions Before Leaving Earth, if it is the book that gives us principles on how to live life, if it is a collection of anecdotes from which we grab moral platitudes to apply, then we will continue to ask what is cultural and what is eternal and to debate the answer.

What if we're asking the wrong question? What if this distinction between eternal and applicable, cultural and irrelevant, isn't a helpful question at all? Questions always frame the possible available answers. Different questions yield a different pool of possible answers.

With this in mind, I conducted my own informal research. I asked pastors, master's of divinity degree holders, and hermeneutics students of God's Word why we think we're supposed to do what the Bible says. I asked the vice president of a major publishing house the same question. I asked conference attendees, members of churches I work with, and district superintendents of major denominations (three different ones). The response was immediate and universal and unanimous: we should do what the Bible says *because it is the inspired Word of God.* There you have it. In the minds of pastors, Christian publishing house executives, book editors, lay leaders, and Bible teachers, mimicking the text is the obvious outflow of inspiration.

I wore those same lenses.

Our premise is that inspiration requires doing what the text says whenever possible, but what if we're wrong? That may be what we have been taught, it may be what is in our heads; but is it really what Scripture teaches? The only passage that uses the word *inspiration*, 2 Timothy 3:16–17, says that the inspired text is profitable for four things—teaching, rebuking, correcting, and training in righteousness. Mimicking the Bible isn't on the list. The Bible is certainly valuable and inspired and relevant, but that's not the question here. The question is, Does inspiration imply mimicking? The answer, I think, is no. Stick with me; I will explain.

ASKING A BETTER QUESTION

On occasion, I go to the eye doctor for a prescription update. And you know what I always find uncanny? How much the human body is able to compensate when under less than ideal conditions, and how it does so without us even knowing it. When do we need a prescription change to our lenses? The easy and obvious answer is when our vision seems to be slipping a bit or things are starting to look a little blurry.

But believe it or not, I'm rarely aware of the slow drift to blurriness or decreased clarity of vision. I need a lens change when I start to get headaches from squinting. I may not even be aware I am squinting or that my vision is blurry, but as my vision begins slipping, my body begins physically compensating for my astigmatism by squinting to change the curvature of my eyeball. After a while it gets to be a real headache. When I do the little eye chart test with the funky lens flipper contraption in front of my face, I'm always amazed at how much better I can see. I had no idea my vision had changed that much without my being aware of it.

I think this may be what has happened with the lenses we use to read the Bible. They aren't serving us too well anymore. We are squinting to the point of getting headaches, but we aren't aware things are blurry. Furthermore, we are unaware that a lens change is even possible.

What if we can get the prescription changed and acquire new, updated lenses by asking a different question? What if the question we have been asking isn't the best question because it limits what we see? What if we pose an alternative question that opens up all sorts of new possibilities?

I think I may have a candidate: *How do we let an ancient text shape our life?* Sounds simple. Pondering how a text shapes a life takes a more macro, flying-at-50,000-feet perspective; the old question compels us to drill down into minutiae. The new question makes the text accessible to the average reader, the old question largely to the specialist. The new question looks at big contours; the old question—what is eternal truth and applies to our lives, and what is cultural and does not—examines the pieces and the parts.

What if we are willing to admit that *the whole text is cultural.* None of the text was written to me, Ron Martoia, in the twenty-first century. In other words, I cannot assume that any of the text has direct application. I am not mandated to build a Noah boat or have a Nicodemus paradigm shift. These two stories surely have implications for my life, and so the question is, What *are* the implications? Inspiration does not mean that what was written to believers in Ephesus in the middle of the first century now magically applies and is to be mimicked by me nearly two thousand years later. So if we admit that the Bible is a text that is entirely cultural, and that none of it was written to us now—*but* we still believe the whole of the Bible is useful for us (à la 2 Timothy 3)—then the question has to do with *how* is it profitable.

This, then, is my quest: to figure out how an ancient text not written to me can shape, mold, impact, dent, contour, and mess with me—and ultimately have authority in my life. The old approach of fishing out the abiding truth and leaving the cultural stuff behind has served its time. We are squinting way too hard; headaches have become way too common. It is time for a lens change.

A new question can provide new options. We will have to be patient with the rebellion in our heads, though. Everything in us loves the way these lenses fit and have been focusing things for us. We love the certainty we claim as we haul in the interpretation of various texts. We have grown accustomed to the modern project of dissecting the text down to little bits and bytes so we can be sure we have captured the exact thoughts of the author. We run pretty confidently with our current lenses, even if the vision they provide is headache inducing and blurry at times. So we will have to suspend judgment long enough to enter into dialogue with some new ideas.

I know the pain of this journey. For a long time I lived in smug certainty. Even though I had unresolved questions, I was relatively sure I had the right method. The right method was yielding pretty good interpretive results, even amidst glaring exceptions. Over time, however, the exceptions grew—as did something even more troubling. I realized the Bible wasn't bringing the life change to me and others the way I thought it should. It was here that the pain of the journey really set in. Previously held assumptions were up for grabs. Unanswered biblical questions such as the ones raised so far, shelved for rainy-day consideration, could no longer be ignored.

What was about to happen was unexpected. In my journey toward a deeper grappling with how the Bible is supposed to work in my life, I underwent a dramatic shift in my view of how we develop as people of faith. I came across a tool for understanding our journey that led to new insights into what was going on inside of me. It was just another one of those "thank you, God, for the resources and mentors you bring into my life at the right time" moments. I have a sneaking suspicion the journey of faith development may go hand in hand with our ability to entertain new metaphors for how the Bible is to shape us.

SEVEN CHAPTER

FAITH AND HUMAN DEVELOPMENT

Exploring My Assumptions

FOR MOST OF my life, I have been under the impression that growth and development come through increased knowledge. I say "under the impression" because I'm not sure I was ever explicitly taught this. Perhaps going to school as a five-year-old and continuing through graduate school had something to do with it—coupled with my early Christian experience of studying the Bible. It is possible that you do not associate growth with knowledge acquisition the way I did, but I would be surprised. Many of my friends and the church members I've worked with show that this association is quite common, even if it is tacit. You might call it another set of lenses or assumptions we have just sitting in a blind spot.

Our church ministry models seem to utilize this blind-spot assumption: give people a myriad of biblical material in the form of extracted timeless propositions and life will go better, God's blessings will ensue, and they will come to know who they are in Christ. Repeat to them the biblical tradition, get them to obey those tenets of the tradition—and they are good to go. The questions they have about life and its meaning, and even about the problem of evil, will get answered. The questions of how relationships are to work, what to believe about a host of social issues, and how to get life to work God's way will all become resolved if you are simply exposed to enough of the Bible. Master the owner's manual for life, and your life will hum.

STAGES OF FAITH

I have just described what James Fowler calls a predictable early stage of faith development.[1] Fowler is a professor of theology and human development and has spent his life studying and articulating how our development as humans and then as Christians unfolds. I have a hunch our ability to entertain new ways of viewing the Bible is intimately tied to the unfolding of our own development. My own journey reflects this, and maybe as I share a bit of my journey, you will begin to grab on to handles for the next stage in your development of seeing how the Bible shapes you.

For Fowler, stages of faith have to do with a general sequential and predictable way of experiencing our faith.[2] Just as we can't skip stages in physical development, neither can we jump over stages in faith development. These faith stages are ways we know and value, and they eventually lead to action. Stages of faith don't reflect as much a hierarchy as they do our ability to hold increasingly greater amounts of complexity, ambiguity, and paradox in tension. Stages of faith represent shifts in the way we know and value; and as we progress, these ways become increasingly complex, holistic, and comprehensive. Each stage shift is a new way of forming meaning and making sense of our world, including the world of faith. Each stage represents a shift in perspective.

We see a larger part of the world and come to make sense of the whole in new and complex ways.

I went on a run in a mountainous area in Arizona recently and took pictures with my phone camera at different intervals. At a thousand feet up the mountain I had a reasonably good view. The terrain was beautiful, and I could see a few of the homes surrounding the area where I had begun my run. As I went another five hundred feet, then another thousand, then another five hundred, my perspective changed. At each turn of the mountain, I could see more and more of the land I had traversed. I had a much more spacious, higher altitude view as well. I could now see the entire development of homes from where I had started, as well as an expansive valley beyond the housing development on one side and a whole new range of mountains that had just come into view on the other side.

I was covering two thousand feet of altitude change, and with those shifts in altitude and the multiple turns and switchbacks, I could see more and more landscape. The higher I got, the more I could see of the shadow side and previously hidden aspects of the mountain range. At the summit, I saw where I had come from, but I could also see entirely different mountains and new housing developments I hadn't even known existed. A higher altitude doesn't make a place superior, but it does provide the setting for a broader view. There is more available landscape to view, a greater amount of complexity to behold—more variety, more beauty, more options.

As we human beings proceed through stages of faith, this is precisely what happens to us. Stages of faith are like high-altitude vantage points. In life and faith, the more I can see, the more complexity I can hold, and the broader the views I have, the wider, more timely, more systematic, and more informed my actions and decisions are likely to become. Increased altitude brings more relevant information, allows connections to be made that were previously unseen, and shows the dynamic and systemic nature of all relationships.

For our interests here, *meaning making* is the key component. When we are in the early stages of faith development, how we make sense of our life, our purpose, God's role, and the Bible are all very different than they are at later stages. How we make sense not only of our lives but events around us — global conditions and catalytic events — all change as we move through stages of faith. Human and faith development is meaning making.[3]

As I briefly describe these stages of faith development and how they influenced my understanding of the Bible, I hope you will encounter some aha moments, as I did. Many people I've talked to have found these insights liberating and encouraging as they have gone through times of vertigo and disequilibrium in not only what they believe but what they understand the role of the Bible to be in their faith development. New lenses allow us to see new things. And a higher altitude gives us a wider panorama for our viewing pleasure.

Primal Faith Pre-Stage and Intuitive/Projective Faith Stage

Fowler says the first stages of faith represent what happens at birth through the toddler stage. We experience our first separation from our mothers and identify with significant others in our world. The primal faith pre-stage and intuitive/projective faith stage deal with how we come to get our bearings in this new world we have entered. Clearly this has a formative effect when it comes to an understanding of who God is, what God is about, and what God is asking of me.

Very early in my development, as I am recognizing that my mother is separate from me, the quality and health of that relationship and separation into an individual self will have a residue that impacts other relationships in unconscious ways. Does it make sense that if I was abandoned, abused, neglected, or hurt in the earliest stages of my growth, it will be hard not to have that pain and emotional scar tissue affect other relationships, including the one I have with God? You can begin to see how critical even early development is for our view of God.

As you read through the descriptions of the next stages, reflect on these questions about how you make sense of your world: How do you make meaning and define who you are? What is your purpose? How do you relate and interact with God? How do you define God? What is your story of stories? What ties all of the subplots and micropieces into an overarching narrative?

Mythic/Literal Faith Stage

Early in our school years, at about six or seven years old, certain things begin to happen cognitively as well as spiritually. In the mythic/literal faith stage, our reasoning power is sufficiently developed so we see the world as more linear, stable, and predictable. We become aware the world appears to be guided by certain laws about how things work. We begin the ability to climb into the worlds of other people around us and notice that they have perspectives different from our own.

Faith at this stage is based on oral storytelling and narrative. The biblical text, in other words, is approached as a collection of stories. Values, morals, and rules are found in these stories and are passed on from the community units of family and faith where we learn what is expected. Identification with the larger units of family, church, and group are the first experiences of God we have. We come to know who we are and how to relate to God as we hear stories of our families' and churches' history with God and each other. While we hear stories and know there is learning value in finding the morals of these stories, we don't yet have what Fowler calls a "story of stories."[4] We don't yet have an overarching narrative that makes sense of the parts. We have no big plot and story line by which the "subchapters" become coherent.

Whatever experience we had early on in our development—the way God was perceived, talked about, and interacted with—has enormous shaping power for the rest of our lives. And if our view of God remains unconscious, then our views and outlook will remain in our blind spot. We don't initially create our view of God. We don't think about it; we don't select what to believe or not believe. We primarily inherit it. This is true in religious and nonreligious settings, in agnostic and atheistic settings. Our environment molds and shapes our knowledge and expectations of God.

At the mythic/literal stage, we begin to realize there are those like us and those not like us. We are part of our tribe, family, church, and story—and someone over there is not. An "us here" versus "them out there" mentality is first experienced at this early stage of development. We see this mentality most obviously on the playground in early grade school. Who do we choose to play kickball, and who do we ignore? Who are the cool kids, and who aren't?

Affiliation is key to our meaning making at this stage of development. We gain a sense of identity from the larger group, whatever that group might be. Loyalty is a significant value at this stage. We have basic rules of life and religion. We learn that it's wrong to lie and to throw stones at cars, and that God expects us to pray before meals and bed. We learn these things in Sunday school, around the dinner table, in a third grade class discussion, on TV, or in playground conversations. Life is concrete and literal.

We see clear signs of mythic/magical thinking here: if you do this, God will do that; if you don't do this, God will do something else. The world of spirit is neat, tidy, literal, and predictable—but also somewhat magical.

This is the domain of mythic/literal development. Some adults can remain here in terms of certain elements of this stage, but most progress at least to the next stage of faith development.

Synthetic/Conventional Faith Stage

Synthetic/conventional faith usually emerges in early adolescence. Something important happens in our cognitive development as we move from simply being able to mentally manipulate concrete objects and things we can observe to being able to construct possibilities and hypotheses. Abstract concepts and imagination ignite to take us into a whole new area of mental experience in which we for the first time experience a sense of self and self-consciousness. We become aware of an interior self, complete with emotions and an ability to look at our own way of relating and our own sense of personality. We not only have awareness of this in ourselves but we assume this is the experience of others as well.

The *synthetic* part of synthetic/conventional has to do with the ability to bring together disparate pieces into a whole. Creating a story of stories is now possible. Taking my life *stories* and beginning to construct a life *story* is a major step in meaning making. For the first time, I bring together values, rules, and a view of God and community that all cohere into a whole. Making meaning of life in general and of my life specifically can now happen in broad contours. A sense of timeline, possible purpose, and even destiny begins here.

The *conventional* part of this stage describes the value, belief, and worldview elements we inherit from those around us. *Inherit* is a good word here because we don't consciously adopt these elements. As members of the family and the faith community, we simply adopt these. We are perhaps being explicitly taught them, but we aren't evaluating whether these elements are good to adopt versus some other set we are considering. Parents, Sunday school teachers, and pastors all give us the stock conventional building blocks they think we need and are thought to be essential to our development. We can modify and manipulate these values and concepts minimally at this stage, but we are unable to critically reflect on them. Here our view of the Bible is formed. What we think the Bible is for, how we are to use it, and just what it tells us all are shaped at this stage.

Many persons spend their entire lives in this synthetic/conventional faith stage. The stock answers, the inherited values and worldview, are satisfying, useful, and functional. Remember, there is no value judgment on one stage being better than another. Different stages have different ways of meaning making. As we make our way through these stages, we are progressing through greater complexity and a growing ability to hold ambiguity and paradox in tension.

If many adults stall here in their development, it's no wonder many of us struggle to understand the Bible in new ways. If this is the stage of faith in which what we understand about God, the Bible, and spiritual life is almost exclusively inherited, then it should be no surprise we are unaware of the many other possible alternatives. This stage of faith is *conventional*. It has conventional, stock, normative answers that are passed on, unquestioned, and adopted. We are wearing lenses, but unaware we are doing so.

I Was an Expert—at Least until Age Thirty-Nine

When I hit thirty-nine and had completed more than fifteen years in ministry, all of my questioning came to a head. I realized there was something incomplete in the way I was approaching the Bible—and maybe it was even worse than simply *incomplete*. Thinking of the Bible as a book full of propositions to make everything work the way God intended just wasn't cutting it. It was dawning on me that I had a definite way of understanding the world and my life—of making meaning—and it wasn't holding up as well as it used to. And yet this was the view of God and the Bible I had inherited in all my schooling, and it is the view I had been teaching for most of my ministry life.

The mechanical, formulaic, computerized approach to applying God's principles was not adding up for me or the people I was serving in ministry. People who faithfully applied the Bible just did not see things work out according to what seemed to be promised. If these propositions were given to make life work together for good and for God, then something was deeply wrong. Too many unanswerable questions were generated by the paradigm I had inherited and was propagating.

When I say the mechanical view was not working, I don't want to leave the impression I or the people I served did not have a relationship with God. The people I was doing life and ministry with had a warm relationship with God. I had formed good rhythms of prayer and meditation. I was employing good Bible reading habits. The classical disciplines were important to me. I want to make clear, though, that when we talk about meaning making and worldview, we are talking about structures in our thinking and view of life so woven into the very way we live that they are by and large quietly hidden from view. Only because I have moved through this stage of development can I see more clearly the view of God I had and the stage of faith I was swimming in. Questions and disruptions are often the catalysts that move us into new stage explorations.

In some Christian circles, when these questions or misgivings arise, you are told to just trust God or exercise faith—or some will even tell you that your questions may be a sign you really aren't "saved." While I have faced only a minimal amount of nay-saying, I *have* faced some, and I know plenty of people who have encountered an onslaught of chastisement. In-between stages are very hard places.

The In-between Place

Anthropologists call in-between space "liminal space." *Limen*, the Latin root for *liminal*, is the word we translate *threshold*. When you are in the threshold of a doorway, you aren't inside the room or outside; you are in between the two. Being in liminal spaces may bring a sense of excitement and newness that is exhilarating; but because we are leaving what is known, familiar, and comfortable and going into foreign, new, and stressful territory, it can also be lonely, disorienting, and discouraging.

Our lives represent more than where we have come from, and we can author our lives through a conscious examination of those things that have been in our blind spots as we begin to see a new array of other possibilities. Self-authoring is a lonely, risky, vertigo-inducing process. For the first time, we come to a place in our development where we are choosing what to hold on to. We are moving from holding on to the hidden things we have inherited to intentionally choosing from a broader palette the things that will help us move into the next stage of life. Messing with what we have inherited is liminal, for sure.

The first time I realized the specific questions I was wrestling with were not the problem—that the framework or lenses into which those questions were inserted was the issue—I was in a liminal space. The way I was approaching the Bible was limiting the scope of the possible answers I could obtain. The certainty elements in my Bible study, the "I am convinced of my position" dimensions, all squared well with a synthetic/conventional level of development. But this particular faith stage only has stock answers available.

Many catechisms, creeds, and statements of faith are efforts to codify, stabilize, indoctrinate, and formalize the key issues we feel should be inculcated in the newbie coming into the faith family. On the flip side, these codified things are better left unquestioned, untweaked, and, even in some church settings, unexplored.

Certainty and Expertise

As I have learned more about adult development, I see why certainty as a value fits into the overall system. I understand its role in my own life far better too. Certainty is a high value in making meaning in early stages of adult faith development. Linear, predictable, cause-and-effect ways of explaining God and the world are normal.

In the days after Hurricane Katrina hit, some religious people carried out a bizarre juxtaposition with regard to God's role in the hurricane. Those with a meaning-making apparatus that homed in on a God who chalks the playing field and smacks anyone who runs outside the baseline were quick to weigh in and let us know that the hurricane reflected God's judgment on the debauchery and the pagan lifestyle of New Orleans. YouTube videos and websites called for citywide repentance and described what happened as a modern-day Sodom-and-Gomorrah event. Note here the random hijacking of a biblical example to justify a perspective within a particular meaning-making scenario. People wanted to make sense of what happened—which isn't a surprising conclusion for people in the conventional stage of faith development who have a fundamentalist view of God.

Other people called for prayer and aid—engendering a compassionate response at a time when fellow human beings were experiencing incredible suffering and loss. Christians who took this approach made sense out of natural disasters in a different fashion, which indicates that their view of both God and the Bible was different.

Boston College professor emeritus Bill Torbert has focused much of his research on stages of leadership development, which has application to our discussion of human development. We learn from Torbert's research that about 75 percent of adults never leave what he calls the Expert stage of development. There are a couple of stages of adult development below Expert and several above, but with so many landing in the Expert stage and never moving, we must dig deeper into what is happening here.[5]

Experts are exactly what they sound like — highly competent in their area and certain of the answers they hold. You cannot persuade an Expert by positioning yourself as a higher-level Expert — because they already know it all. Experts are not able to do good self-reflection. They live in their world of cause and effect and logic, and they grind out the right answers. Experts believe they have an objective view of the world — and it is the right view. Experts feel a need to convince others of their position.

Remember, the Expert category represents a stage of development. It is not a statement about the mastery of a skill or body of knowledge, which is the way the word is commonly used. A full-time stay-at-home parent can be an Expert, as can the logical engineer. The home chef who watches *Iron Chef America* can be an Expert. The artist can be. The religious fanatic surely can be. The Expert stage doesn't have to do with a knowledge base per se but with how one makes meaning and sense of the world. Experts feel a need for certainty, answers, coherent explanations, cause and effect, and an ability to execute within that world. These are stages in the development of the self.

Noticing any parallels here? Just like Fowler's stages of faith, these stages of development are sequential and unavoidable. Nor do they imply any inferiority. Toddler development isn't inferior to adolescent development, but you can't get to adolescence without first being a toddler.

I refer to this work of Torbert, which is only a representative sample of a large field of research, to help us see that the Expert stage of human development is roughly the same as the synthetic/conventional stage of faith development. The level of certainty, confidence in objectivity, rightness, and completeness of a person's worldview is very similar. And those of us who have experienced this stage can smile because we know how true this is!

Seminary made me an Expert. Pastoral ministry expected me to be an Expert as well. Answers, solutions, interpretations, insights, mastery of Hebrew and Greek words, social analysis, cultural commentary—all of these are the domain of the omnicompetent pastor. And I was one—at least during my Expert stage. And Expert pastors tend to develop Expert churches with disciples who are growing up to be Experts.

When I had the dawning during that several-month aha period at thirty-nine years of age, I experienced the rude awakening that Expert wasn't the goal. I didn't have language for what was going on yet, but I did realize that something was happening.

I can easily identify the Expert stage of development because I went through it. I was dogmatic, right, well reasoned, articulate, convincing, unmoved, resourced, and scholar quoting—all standard earmarks of the Expert. More than that, however, I made sense of my life and my image of self by becoming and dispensing my expertise. Even though I was asking questions that had the potential to carry me outside of the stock answers I had inherited, I remained a card-carrying Expert.

Synthetic/conventional faith will be most appealing to adults at the Expert stage of human development. At this stage there are expected answers—the tried-and-true dispensed by other Experts in my clan, tribe, church, or denomination.

My charismatic renewal group was full of adults who were at the Expert stage of human development: they dispensed the standard charismatic answers and end-time scenarios. The Catholic Church surely was Expert: the pope was Expert number one, and Expertness filtered down through the ranks to the local priest. And there is no doubt my Presbyterian church was Expert: we recited creeds, had a standard order of service every Sunday, and held definite positions on most ethical and social issues—right down to the same chair we sat in every week. Predictable, certain, routine, and unwavering.

I am sure you are doing a little self-reflection as you read these descriptions. I think it is almost impossible to read about categories like these and not want to try to understand where we each fit and how we move from stage to stage. For me, it was helpful to realize that we have emotions, maybe even pain, associated with movement into and through various stages. Growth of an individuating sort is not easy or popular, but it is a necessary part of the development process. We don't need to be afraid. Transition between stages is a liminal experience!

Individuative/Reflective Faith Stage

Individuative/reflective faith is a watershed stage. We have not only brought some minimal skills of synthesis from the previous stage, but we've now added the ability to critically examine the images, values, and beliefs we have tacitly adopted or inherited. We can now ask questions about the lenses we are wearing, when before we had no idea we had lenses on.

Harvard professor Robert Kegan (adult learning and human development) explains this transition by noting that we grow when we move material from subject to object. Subject material is the stuff we hold tacitly; it's simply part of the way we view the world. When we come to learn something new, we slot the new knowledge into the cubbyholes or worldview we unconsciously operate with throughout our day. Kegan calls this *informational learning*, information that is added to the current form of our mind and contributes to the affirmation and confirmation of the very worldview being held. Adhering to informational learning has significant implications for our view of God and the Bible. Much of my learning in my adolescent days (in the three religious venues I have already described) was of the informational sort.

When we move material that is subject to us—part of our lenses, part of the structure of how we see the world—and move it out in front of us as an object to explore and examine, we are potentially changing the way we view what we know. Kegan calls this *transformational learning*, a type of learning that makes the mind more spacious, complex, and able to deal with multiple demands and uncertainty. When we can step back and critically reflect on something previously hidden to us, transformation occurs.[6]

Fowler's individuative/reflective stage displays this shifting of material from subject to object—a shift occasioned by a variety of elements leading to a questioning of what has been inherited. This can be a painful and difficult time. Up to this point, our sense of self has been inherited from and defined by the larger family, tribe, or community. We were part of a whole, and our identity was derived from it. Individuating faith requires that I step out and examine the larger group beliefs, values, and ethics I have always held. Ridicule, skepticism, and frowning by those in the larger group—whether family, church, or denomination—is not uncommon. Lack of conformity is perceived at times as rebellion, excessive inquisitiveness, disrespect of "our history," and even defection from the faith.

The individual entering this stage has to "begin to be and act from a new quality of self-authorization."[7] The person at this stage is saying, "I am going to reflect on [hence the stage name] what I have inherited, and I am going to decide whether this is still the best way for me to proceed in my own growth. It's OK, even if my family or church doesn't like my decisions, because my sense of self isn't rooted in my history alone; I am going to take responsibility for authoring some of it myself." The person entering this stage is usually at least in his or her late thirties or into their forties. The reasons are several, but the most obvious is that life experience has provided the opportunity to try on for size all of our inherited "clothing," and we are now deciding whether it is worth investigating a new wardrobe.

Journey into Self-Reflective Faith

I had misgivings along the way about how I was using the Bible in my teaching and preaching, but I could always find an excuse: everybody does it; this passage has traditionally been preached this way; this is what I was taught; this is all I know. All of these things would roll through my mind at different times in my preaching journey, but those unanswerable, intractable questions became acute at this stage.

I distinctly remember the time I was preparing for a series on stewardship/giving and wrestling about whether it was appropriate to use Malachi 3 as a way to convince people that the church was entitled to at least 10 percent of their income. This wrestling represented a catalytic moment for me in terms of moving into a new stage of faith development.

"Will a mere mortal rob God? Yet you rob me.

"But you ask, 'How are we robbing you?'

"In tithes and offerings. You are under a curse—your whole nation—because you are robbing me. Bring the whole tithe into the storehouse, that there may be food in my house. Test me in this," says the LORD Almighty, "and see if I will not throw open the floodgates of heaven and pour out so much blessing that there will not be room enough to store it. I will prevent pests from devouring your crops, and the vines in your fields will not drop their fruit before it is ripe," says the LORD Almighty. "Then all the nations will call you blessed, for yours will be a delightful land," says the LORD Almighty.

MALACHI 3:8 – 12

It's easy to forget the context of Malachi 3, but let me give you some of the meanderings that were going on inside of me. These words are obviously addressed to Israel as a people and are referring to their having disobeyed a command given earlier in their history, hence the charge of "robbing." The cost of not tithing here is that the whole nation is under a curse.

This was my thought process as I wrestled with how to apply this text. How can an injunction to Israel as a nation, with a curse issued for disobedience, be translated, with a one-to-one correspondence, into sermons for the church? Furthermore, if 10 percent is the magic number, not 9 or 12, then why isn't the tithe talked about in the New Testament? If we are operating on the "if the book says it, mimic it" model of interpretation, then this is certainly enforceable. But is this really legitimate? I realize that many have preached this as *the* road to the financial blessing of God, but is it a good way to do the interpretive task?

There is a supposed principle at work, and the translation of this principle into the context we are now in warrants such an application. Really? I know it is easy to pick "giving" texts in the New Testament — passages about giving generously, according to ability. But to single out Malachi 3:10 as a way to let the baseline of our giving be 10 percent of our income — is that really a fair and appropriate usage of the text? And are we willing to preach with the same rigor and persuasion a curse on our lives if we don't do the 10 percent full monty?

This was part of my journey into being honest and reflective about my faith. I had been buying the stock answers of the faith and the Bible.

These thoughts about tithing and Malachi 3 illustrate the unanswered cracks surfacing at this stage in my growth and journey. My experience as a Christian, pastor, and now transformational architect for churches and leaders is that there is one of two outcomes when you enter the individuative/reflective stage of faith: either you reach forward toward a reconfigured faith that is more complex and nuanced, less dogmatic, and marked by deep humility, or you become lost in a cynical skepticism that despairs of ever knowing anything, which leads to a distancing of yourself from Christianity.

Our view of the Bible plays a big role in this growth process. For me and many others I work with, the Bible has been the static repository of timeless truths — and now all of a sudden, as our meaning-making structures shift, so does our confidence in the stock answers that were once satisfying. I'm not saying this implies a step back from the significance of the Bible, questioning whether it is inspired or valuable. What I am realizing is *how* the Bible is profitable for teaching, rebuking, correcting, and training in righteousness (2 Timothy 3:16 – 17).

My changes in faith development were provoked by Bible questions, which pushed me deeper into my faith, which pushed me into a changed and deeper relationship with Scripture.

Conjunctive Faith Stage

When people make their way into the individuative/reflective stage, they are preparing for a new stage of self-understanding and God-understanding called the conjunctive faith stage—a stage rarely experienced before midlife. The phrase *conjunctive faith* comes from the fourteenth-century work of Nicholas of Cusa, whose *De docta ignorantia* used the idea of God as the *coincidentia oppositorum*, the "coincidence of opposites"—the being and place where all contradictions and opposites meet and are reconciled. In this stage, contradictions, opposites, and paradox in self, society, and even God can all come together and live in peaceful tension. Something of a developmental milestone or watershed is reached here. For the first time, the goal of certainty is fully relinquished, and a new way of understanding emerges.

James Fowler has a helpful insight here:

> The hard-won integrity of the individuative stage is based on a clear sense of reflective identity, a firm set of ego boundaries, and a confident regard for one's conscious sense of self as though it were virtually exhaustive of one's total selfhood. The experience of reaching midlife (age thirty-five and beyond) for some people marks the onset of new dimensions of awareness that can precipitate the movement to a new stage, the stage of conjunctive faith. In this transition, the firm boundaries of the previous stage begin to become porous and permeable.[8]

Certainty gives way to humility. The premium value of knowing it all and having everything screwed down gives way to a chastened rationality that is now tempered by intuitional and spiritual rumblings that occur at suprarational levels. By this stage in life we have lived as adults for a couple of decades. We have seen death, maybe that of close friends. We have seen our kids become teenagers and young adults, and we have seen parents grow old and die. The cumulative impact of these events causes us to wonder about and question whether the pat standard answers are adequate to bear the burden of real life. For some people they are; for others they are not.

In this place of reflection we come to see that some questions are simply unanswerable. What would previously have been a disquieted mind—torn by not getting all the answers to cohere—now gives way to a mind of quiet peace that can hold ambiguity, mystery, unanswerables, paradox, and the unknown. In some ways, God may seem bigger at this stage of faith—a God whose magnitude is appropriate to the magnitude of life and global issues.

Fowler notes four hallmarks of the movement into this stage of faith.

First, *a growing awareness that maturity entails holding a number of polarities in tension*—being both young and old, feminine and masculine, rational and intuitional, and, maybe most significant, having both a conscious and unconscious self that fuels more behavior than we ever thought possible.

Second, *a shift in our view of truth*. More than all the other earmarks of transition, this one is significant because of how we have viewed and now wrestle with viewing the Bible. Truth is felt to be more complex and not nearly as dogmatic and certain. The clearcut categories of previous stages give way to a multidimensionality and a realization that our previous certainty was simply assumed and yet was the result of only one vantage point. When the perspective changes, how we view everything in the world around us changes too. We therefore have to approach truth from multiple perspectives simultaneously if we want the full story.

Changing our understanding of truth is not a denial of truth, as those who have failed to move toward the individuative/reflective stage often charge. Universal truths still exist, and the Bible is still a true document.

The shift in truth we speak of here reflects the insights we have received from quantum mechanics. The distinction between the viewer (me) and the viewed (the object out there) is really an illusion. What I bring to the table of viewing already influences the outcome of what I see. This is the big insight in quantum physics. When we touch the book we are reading or the chair we are sitting in, we have a sense that these are "solids." When I touch them, I sense that they are hard. But this hardness is deceptive. When we go down to the microscopic level of the atoms that make up the book or chair, we discover far more space in the atom than parts containing mass. In other words, what feels solid to the touch is almost nonexistent to microscopic sight. To put it in more common terms, things are not always as they appear.

Quantum mechanics helps us realize how the presence of the observed impacts the behavioral outcome of the observed. Viewer and viewed create an event in which the two things simultaneously create what comes to be known. As we look at the most fundamental building blocks of existence, do we see packets of energy or waves of light? Quantum mechanics says it will depend on which tool you use to answer that question; in other words, the answer could be either one or both! Objective certainty is an illusion.[9]

Third, *a move into a new naïveté.* The previous stage of deconstruction and analysis gives way to a new appreciation of the deeper value of the symbols, creeds, and texts that previously were atomized and dissected. Because these things are now viewed from multiple perspectives and layers, they are reengaged with a new value and life. A new vantage point brings a new wholeness and holism. This third stage provides a springboard for the final hallmark.

Fourth, *a genuine openness to the truth found in other faith traditions.* Be careful here. This hallmark does not imply uncritical acceptance of anything and everything. Rather, Fowler says this is "a disciplined openness to the truths of those who are 'other,' based precisely on the experience of a deep and particular commitment to one's own tradition and the recognition that truth requires a dialectical interplay of such perspectives."[10]

I sense this is a full-on embrace of the "all truth is God's truth" principle.[11] A lot of things are true in a lot of sources and disciplines outside of Christianity and outside of the Bible. The Bible does not have a higher-grade or purer form of truth. The Bible has truth, as do other sources; and wherever we have truth, we have something authored and therefore authorized by God. I say that not to bat at a straw man but because I often hear the statement, "There is Bible truth — the true truth — and then there are other forms of truth that rank somewhere further down the pecking order." Calculus and poetry, Copernicus and Dickens, dentists' knowledge about teeth and tooth decay, and the love we claim we feel for each other all have truth — a truth that is one and the same as the truth in the Bible. It cannot be otherwise.

I think this is Fowler's intent. In this stage of conjunctive faith, we realize there is truth in other faith traditions. We can now see these truths and learn from them without giving up on our own tradition, which is the unique province and domain of conjunctive faith. I do not believe this means I have to give up on the distinctives of Christianity, nor have I. But it does mean I have moved past the place where I need to assert my rightness and another's wrongness and instead have come to a place of listening and mutual learning.

NEW LENSES AND DIFFERENT STREET CORNERS

During these steps in my journey, I was coming to grips with a shift that was happening in my worldview. I could see how it had been formed early on, and now it was undergoing a reformation. If any research has been done on whether shifts in stages of faith entail shifts in the way we view the Bible, I can't find it. I do have some hunches, however—hunches that grow out of my personal journey and the ministry trek I have been on with hundreds of leaders.

I've already told you about the shift I underwent at age thirty-nine, but there is more to the story that may shed light. In hindsight, it is easy to see I was moving into a developmental shift. When I was facing the challenge of faithfully preaching Malachi 3, I was confronting a much larger issue than just a passage in the book of Malachi. I was tired of the weary, rutted, and routinized platitudes extracted from biblical stories as if they were another one of Aesop's fables. Such an approach not only didn't work in a simple cause-and-effect way but also didn't seem faithful to the text, at least not anymore.

I returned to an old conversation we had in Study back in my high school days—a conversation that was repeated in graduate school and many times since as a pastor. The conversation centered around why there are four gospels, but especially the Synoptics —Matthew, Mark, and Luke (so named because they see [optic] together [syn]). The Synoptic Gospels see the same basic material but from different vantage points. When you investigate—taking note, for example, of the differing order of the temptation narratives in Matthew and Luke or each gospel's differing view of the disciples —the differences in the Synoptics are theologically substantial.

Apparently those responsible for the canon selection felt it was important to have four vantage points on the life of Jesus. The four gospels offer four distinct viewpoints on the life of Jesus. The differences in the accounts are precisely what make each gospel valuable. To use our current metaphor, each gospel writer had a different set of lenses through which he viewed the life of Jesus.

Let's think about a car accident. Two cars approach a busy intersection and collide, someone calls 911, the police arrive, and the interviewing process of the eyewitnesses begins. If a police officer goes to at least one or two people on each of the four street corners to get their take on the accident, which corner do you think will have the best vantage point or be most accurate or have "the most truth?" I'm guessing you would quickly realize that not one of the corners could have "seen" all that happened in the accident. Someone on one corner may have seen a dog jump out into the street, and they believe that this dog caused car #1 to swerve and hit car #2. Someone on another corner may be convinced that the light was red and that the accident was caused by one of the drivers running the red light.

As all the interviews are pieced together, a composite starts to emerge that clearly shows that not one onlooker had a fully omniscient vantage point. And there is even more to the story: we may find out when we interview the drivers that one of them fell asleep at the wheel, had a seizure, or glanced down to read a text message, only to swerve into the other car and cause the accident—an explanation trumping and invalidating the "went through a red light" vantage point or "swerved to miss the dog" theory. So we might say that the gospel writers had different vantage points, even inspired vantage points, but not omniscient ones.

The point is this: I have been one of the onlookers of the biblical story. I have been on one of the street corners with a particular viewpoint. I have been quite convinced my perspective is better than anyone else's on any of the other three corners. After all, my vision wasn't obstructed. I was actually watching as everything happened. I am convinced no one saw any more than I did. I have gone to seminary, earned degrees, studied the Bible, and read other people's opinions too—albeit mostly those who were on the same street corner as me.

Here is what I have been learning over the last few years: My confidence in the swerved-to-miss-the-dog theory might be wrong. It sure looked that way to me, but when the news circulated that one of the drivers had a stroke, I had to revise the very certain and complete interview I gave the policeman. My theory in this particular case, I came to find out, was incomplete. I wasn't wrong per se; it was simply that I had *an incomplete vantage point* without all the facts.

The street-corner illustration is a good picture of my journey with the biblical text. Without Fowler's insights, however, I think I might not only be stuck on the same corner but also be frustrated as to why people cannot see how right my vantage point is.

We all live on our little corners of the interpretive world. We are often unaware that others have equally valid, though different, viewpoints (think gospel writers here)—sometimes with a more accurate and faithful-to-the-text viewpoint. The lenses I have worn for so long have been fine for a leg of the journey. But like all prescription lenses, they need an update from time to time. The text isn't in need of updating; but the lenses I am using are, and the corner I was standing on doesn't need to be a place of permanent residence.

EIGHT CHAPTER

VIEW OF GOD/VIEW OF SCRIPTURE

Dancing behind the Scenes

IN A VERY real sense, my views of the world, God, and the Bible were changing. My worldview was in flux. The term *worldview* is thrown around a lot, so let me be clear what I mean when I use it. The most helpful observation about worldview I've found comes from N. T. Wright, who helps us come to grips with how our understanding of God and the Bible are formed and guides us to an important insight on how those two dance together.[1]

Worldviews have to do with our presuppositions about our culture or society — ideas about how the world works that come to us without thought. We don't think these things through as we adopt them. As I have said, we inherit them, and at the early age they are being formed we aren't even aware there are alternatives. Those of us who are Christ-followers have definite presuppositions — though not always explicit to our minds — about how things should be.

According to N. T. Wright, four dimensions comprise all worldviews.

- First, *worldviews provide the stories, and even the story of all the little stories, about how we view reality.* For instance, if I think there is a God, then how I view circumstances and life is very different from the view I hold if my assumption is there is no God.

- Second, *these stories and story of stories provide the framework for how we answer life's big questions:* How did we get here? Is there a purpose to our existence? Is the world a friendly or hostile place? How is all this going to turn out? How is the world going to end?

- Third, *these questions are answered but are often symbolized as well.* Certain festivals, artifacts, and events remind us of the worldview and the stories that answer the key questions. Our Fourth of July celebration is a great example. The American flag, fireworks, visits to Washington, D.C., and the various memorials are symbols pointing to a larger national story that give us as Americans an identity and solidarity as a people. Think of the many symbols and festivals of the children of Israel that commemorated release from slavery and entry into the Promised Land, for instance.

- Fourth, *worldviews include what is typically called* praxis — a fancy word referring to how we are to interact in the world, what our customary practices are. Building on the above illustration, a praxis piece of our worldview, good or bad, is that America as a land of opportunity gives us the option to pursue our own happiness through career-path choices, making money, becoming independent of our parents, and starting our own family if we wish. These are all parts of this worldview component that explains how we *are* in the world.[2]

When we take all four elements and put them together, we have a fairly comprehensive way of viewing the world, answering questions, making meaning, and living in the world around us. If we change the time period and go back in history, the worldview and elements comprising it will change. This holds true for different cultures as well. The four elements look very different for a man in Soweto, South Africa, than for a wealthy businesswoman in Singapore.

WHICH COMES FIRST?

I think most of us want to say that we believe what we believe because we are "people of the Book" who allow it to shape our understanding of God. But which comes first — our view of God and then our approach to Scripture, or our approach to Scripture and then our view of God? Does what we read in the Bible shape our view of God or do we approach the Bible through our understanding of who we think God is? A classic chicken-and-the-egg question.

Author David Kelsey would say that our view of God and view of the Bible are formed at the same time and in the same way.[3] Kelsey helps us see that it is impossible to have a view of the Bible that hasn't been informed by a certain view of God and that it works the other way around as well. Our view of God informs the way we handle the Bible. So our views of God and the Bible work in a back-and-forth dance that are mutually defining.

Where then do our views of God and the Bible come from?

As we think about what we have learned about stages of faith, we can anticipate the answer. The Christian community is often where we get our first taste of God and the Bible. Kelsey suggests that each believer makes an imaginative construction about what God, the Bible, and Christianity are like based on their first introduction into the Christian community.[4] The naïveté with which we come into these first experiences makes it nearly impossible for these to be anything but profoundly shaping and foundational.

As I interacted with Kelsey's work, I learned that I have indeed *inherited* my views – and two things in particular: my views of God impacted my view of the Bible, and what I learned about the role of the Bible impacted my views of God. This has great practical significance for me, and it is part of the journey I'm on right now.

I have come to appreciate there is much about God I will never understand. And while it may sound stupid, there were times in my life when I thought it was my job to exhaustively understand God and tell everyone everything they needed to know. That posture created in me a sense that mystery needed resolution. Pain and suffering needed explanations, if not solutions. I have come to realize that mystery exists and, due to the magnitude of God, is not to be resolved (think of Job here). Pain and suffering may not be explainable in a broken, infected world. These maturing faith postures helped to move me from being the answer man, with everything figured out, to someone less concerned with explanations and more concerned about living in mystery and being fully present in the midst of suffering.

PRINCIPLES ARE SUPPOSED TO "WORK"

I have already shared how my mechanical and predictable principles of the universe impacted both my view of God and the Bible. I realize my experience isn't universal, but it certainly isn't isolated. In a mechanical world with a God who set it up that way, we look for the rules and the key truths, which are hidden in stories. Hence, we take "the moral of the story" approach we adopted from children's literature (Goldilocks, the Big Bad Wolf):

- short pithy sayings such as those found in Proverbs: "Commit to the LORD whatever you do, and he will establish your plans" (16:3). "In their hearts human beings plan their course, but the LORD establishes their steps" (16:9). *Give your plans to the Lord, and he will establish your path*—a good rule to know. Craft some plans, commit them to God, and he will make it happen.

- laments and songs written by David: "Take delight in the LORD and he will give you the desires of your heart" (Psalm 37:4).

You can imagine how I applied that verse from Psalm 37 in my life. I did undergraduate work in Tulsa, Oklahoma, the hotbed of the Word of Faith movement. Psalm 37:4 is well known among that group. If you genuinely delight in God, so you are taught, you can expect and plan on the desires of your heart being fulfilled. In a sermon given by a famous TV personality who came to my school to speak in chapel, he compared Psalm 37:4 to making a wish and blowing out the candles on a birthday cake. We delight in the Lord, he said, when we close our eyes in adoration and worship of God. During this time of delighting we present to God the desires of our hearts; we are making a wish. And then when we blow out the candles in faith, we wait for the realization of our wishes, the desires of our hearts. All this *seems* relatively harmless—until a human life is at stake.

People put their faith in Scripture verses to "work" as they understand them, and when they don't work according to expectation, we will be disappointed—or worse. Brett, a college student friend of mine, almost lost his brother to sheer parental foolishness. The parents "took God at his Word." They claimed Mark 11:23–24 and prayed for their very sick son in a prayer meeting one night. No problem with that. But they felt that to take him to a doctor would show lack of faith, and so they refused to seek medical treatment for their son—and nearly lost him. Friends of the family confronted the parents, and on their son's near deathbed, the parents finally consented to take him to the hospital.

Tearfully, Brett shared the confusion and pain of the ordeal. As he was growing up, he had trusted his parents and had been taught to trust God. He saw their faithful hearts, even if they were wrongheaded. During his freshman year in college, he entered a state of confusion when it came to God and the Bible—and authority, for that matter. How far do you trust parents when to do so seems so wrong? Yet how can you trust a God who, when "taken at his Word," doesn't appear to be coming through? Brett had decided to enroll in a BA program in New Testament Literature and was hoping to come to grips with some of his exasperation.

Here is another vivid example of uncertainty about how to understand things in context. Brett wasn't just trying to figure out what was for "them back there" and what is for us now on a *theoretical* level; his very life was affected. Brett's parents saw Mark 11:23 – 24 as exclusively an encouragement directly to them to say to the mountain of their son's illness, "Go, throw yourself into the sea" (Mark 11:23). He had been confused, frustrated, and nearly shipwrecked in faith ever since this traumatic faith event. I'm sure you can see how this was catalytic for moving Brett from the synthetic/conventional faith stage to the individuative/reflective stage, where he began to ask hard, probing, even doubting questions because the stock arsenal of answers just didn't hold up any longer.

Sounds outlandish, doesn't it? But it is a true story, and a formative one as well. When you see God as someone who created humanity to play by a heaven-given rule book called the Bible, how is it possible not to see God as anything but a heavenly umpire calling balls and strikes, balks, and outs.

MODERN-DAY SHAMANISM

My views of God and the Bible arose in interaction with each other and were the basis for how I made meaning. And this is also how I made sense of my pastoral role. I was the dispenser of the rules from the rule book. I was the master rule book interpreter.

My dear friend Joe Lengel is one of my favorite dialogue partners when it comes to theological and philosophical questions and how they affect the way people grow. He used a metaphor that helped me understand more about our dysfunctional approach to our view of the Bible. Joe told me that all cultures have had shamans or shamanlike figures.

Shamanism refers to a range of traditional beliefs and practices concerned with communication with the spirit world. A practitioner of shamanism is known as a shaman. There are many variations of shamanism throughout the world; following are beliefs shared by all forms of shamanism:

- Spirits exist, and they play important roles both in individual lives and in human society.
- The shaman can communicate with the spirit world.
- Spirits can be good or evil.
- The shaman can treat sickness caused by evil spirits.
- The shaman can employ trance-inducing techniques to incite visionary ecstasy.[5]

When we think about shamanism, we tend to look toward animistic and tribal cultures. But the first-century mystery religions were all about incantations, about appeasing and pleasing the gods with the right chants and formulas. The whole model is based on Gnosticism, which asserts that you must have a correct knowledge base to be "in"; without this base you are an outsider. If you say the secret password, prayer, or chant, you are an insider and the gods will respond appropriately.

Some Sunday morning worship services, Joe told me, seem to have adopted this model—practicing a modern-day dispensing of magical formulas. Joe even pointed out that in some strands of Christianity people use recitation of various Bible verses to ward off evil spirits or to garner the favor of God so he will act on their behalf. This isn't relationship with God; this is modern-day shamanism.

Joe's point was he feels people in congregations often look to a pastor as a sort of shaman. He said, "They want us to play the intermediary. They are highly dependent, if not codependent. They want us to give them 'the four steps to this, the eight keys to that, and the five insights for the other thing.'"

I had never thought of it that way before, but I instantly resonated. Much of my preaching and teaching had once been about dispensing the "keys" to make it all work right. When I look at much of the Christianity I am familiar with, I think Joe's observation warrants consideration. He said to me, "We have to break the codependency of congregations and pastors. We are in danger of moving Christianity into the realm of magic and incantation more than we care about introducing people into relationship."

Are we in danger of being more Gnostic than Christian? Was I in my pastoral role contributing to people looking to me as a Christian shaman and at God in a sort of "heavenly umpire" way rather than in a relational way?

The Old Testament scholar Walter Brueggemann would agree with Joe's assessment, though he approaches it from a different angle. Brueggemann says we need a text that operates from a higher ceiling than that of the congregation and a longer horizon than that of the preacher.[6] And he says this for the same reasons as Joe. We have been hijacked by the modern world, where rules, principles, and propositions have explained how everything works neatly—including God. We have an authoritative text, to be sure, but it isn't the biblical text; it is the text of the Enlightenment.

The Enlightenment gave us a particular way of seeing the world—predictable, mechanical, technological, with causes that have expected effects. Problems are to be solved by thinking and by rightly applying the right principles. Nothing is really impossible; it's just not fully understood yet. Everything will eventually yield to human brilliance and sovereignty.

When we see the world this way, it is hard to operate with a view of God and the Bible that isn't deeply colored by this worldview. Brueggemann says this text of the Enlightenment has become the normative narrative permeating the consciousness of the Western believer and unbeliever alike. The first tenet of this Enlightenment "text" that informs the mind of every American is the assumption that a reasonable and technical solution to every problem of life exists so that " 'research and development' are the order of the day."[7] He concludes his discussion of "the dominant script":

> I believe this text that we already have [the Enlightenment text]—which is dangerous to criticize in public—is deeply embedded in the church and in our listening apparatus. The power of this text shows up in an excessive theological conservatism that has transposed fidelity into

certitude and believes that if we go deep enough we will find certitudes that are absolutes about morality as about theology, as though somewhere there are rational formulations that will powerfully veto the human ambiguities so palpable among us.[8]

Wow! Brueggemann connects our reading of the Bible with a hidden set of lenses called "the Enlightenment" that make certainty the premium value and finding solutions to life's problems the goal. So powerfully is this agenda rooted in the psyche of the believer that we ignore the ambiguities all around us that don't yield to our rule keeping and application of "the six keys to . . ."

Maybe you can see in my journey some of your own experiences. If you do share with me the lenses I had been wearing (even if the shamanism example is a bit jolting), then you might be asking these questions: Isn't this *the* view though? If the Bible isn't a rule book for playing the game of life, or an owner's manual to make everything hum, then what are the alternatives?

There are alternatives not only in how we view the Bible but also in how we view God—a God untamed by our own discomfort with unpredictability and a text less ordered but full of mystery and paradox. We will look at these alternatives next.

SHIFTING OUR VIEW OF THE BIBLE

Seeing the Snapshot in Time

WE WILL HAVE to playfully entertain some new metaphors for understanding how Scripture shapes our lives if we are going to move beyond those we are most familiar with and therefore most comfortable with.

One of the massive books I read in my advanced hermeneutics class said this about metaphors: "If metaphor, therefore, presents *possibility* rather than *actuality* it is arguable that metaphoric discourse can open up new understanding more readily than purely descriptive or scientific statement."[1] So I say let's ask some questions about the questions we are asking. Let's entertain some new ideas and metaphors that may help us understand a better way to let God's unruly narrative called Scripture loose in our lives. And let's become aware of the lenses we are wearing. The biblical text must be freed to speak to us outside of the medical, mechanical, therapeutic, and self-help texts that permeate our head space.

AN EVOLUTIONARY TRAJECTORY

One of the most dramatic realizations on my journey in the last several years was coming to grips with the fact that the Bible is a record of a bunch of snapshots in time. We have sixty-six books written over roughly 1,500 years in multiple languages to multiple cultures, and each book represents a freeze-frame photo of a particular faith community engaging their questions with their understanding of God in their social context. Each snapshot is about a particular people who have particular ways of doing life. These cultural snapshots of different biblical peoples contain historic peoples and situations with certain sanitation systems, drinking water solutions, views of medicine and sexuality, political systems, ways of dealing with crime, appropriate dress codes, cusswords, and cultural taboos that are hidden from our eyes.

For example, the Stone Age people in the Tower of Babel building project in Genesis 11 have a particular understanding of God, one appropriate to their context and development. In Genesis 12, usually dated somewhere closer to the Bronze Age, we see Abraham engaging with an understanding of God quite different than the story just a chapter earlier but at least a thousand years earlier chronologically. Interestingly, if these accounts are written down by Moses, which is the earliest authorship that anyone has suggested, Moses is writing somewhere about a thousand years after the Abraham narratives. The point is that the events of the Bible are not only from vastly different epochs than ours; the authors who recorded them are also in vastly different contexts than some of the things they are writing about. I know these aren't particularly profound observations, but here is why they are important.

We have somehow come to conclude that the Bible is able to speak directly to us, ahistorically, without significant translation into our culture. And I don't mean Hebrew to English or Greek to English translation. We look at a passage of Scripture without recognizing that it resides within a particular historical time frame or era or epoch that renders the commands (or following someone's example) inappropriate to our time. For instance, people who lived in 800 BC would have had primitive views of sanitation systems. What would make us think that their view of God and interactions with God were not equally primitive? Why would we think they would have had twenty-first-century sensibilities about God and their relationship with that God but would lean toward the archaic, mythical, or magical in every other part of their worldview? This observation is one of the most important and profound I have wrestled with on my journey to understanding the Bible.

Some things certainly appear to be easily applicable without much cultural or historical translation. Take Proverbs 17:27, for instance: "Those who have knowledge use words with restraint, and those who have understanding are even-tempered." Proverbs by their very genre are pithy—often ahistorical and acultural— maxims ready for application (or that is at least how they read to us). And we should note that if God had wanted this ready-to-serve format, he could have given us a Bible full of Proverbs-type ahistorical information. But most of the Bible comes to us in other genres, in literary flavors that do not have instant applicability. Historical narrative, story, myth, and even teaching texts simply aren't always able to bear a one-to-one correspondence from that cultural context or historical time period to the one in which we live.

I am sure no sane person today in our country would consider sacrificing his or her son or daughter, no matter how powerful the dream, vision, or trance. Why? Nothing in our era, experience, or church background would make that sort of thing plausible to us. And yet Abraham is held up as a premier example of faith for the very act of trusting God—that even if Abraham went ahead and killed Isaac, God would raise Isaac from the dead (Hebrews 11:17–19).

Abraham lived during the Bronze Age, an era when child sacrifice to the gods was acceptable. We recognize there is something unique about the time period of Abraham, and so we do not get hung up on the fact he was asked to kill his son. In my experience though, this is rarely discussed from the pulpit, and my guess is it is because we are embarrassed that the text never addresses the glaring issue that Abraham is invited to be a murderer. Was God really OK with that scenario? Would God, even as a test, ask one of us to kill one of our kids? We read the story unmoved by what in our time period seems barbaric and certainly nothing the God we serve would condone—at least not today.

In our part of the world, we don't engage in such practices anymore because religion, like all social constructs and institutions, is on an evolutionary trajectory. We don't do child sacrifice. We don't sell everything we have and hold the proceeds commune style for everyone else to use when they need to. We don't have household slaves.

Slavery in earlier civilizations was considered permissible, even an essential part of the social fabric—in the history of the United States as well. Does this mean in earlier times slavery was OK from God's point of view? I doubt it. God has not changed, but the social setting in which we live out our Christianity has dramatically changed in the last two hundred years, not to mention the changes over the last two thousand. We would consider it unethical, immoral, and illegal to have slaves. But don't forget that the New Testament gives guidance on how slaves and masters are to interact.[2] Are these biblical statements an admission that God endorses slavery? That argument was made by American slave-holders wanting to justify slave ownership and propagation of the institution. We realize that slavery is one of those oppressive social constructs thankfully left in our past due to the changing patterns of culture in all societies over time.

My point is this: Our understandings of God and the Bible are not ahistorical; they are deeply conditioned by our historical situatedness. It cannot be otherwise. I don't think this observation is original at any level. But the implications of this observation rarely seem to be taken into account as we do our biblical reading.

We see Old Testament passages where God ruthlessly directs people to invade a land and destroy every living thing.[3] The cumulative effect of such passages is a view of God as bloodthirsty, militant, and genocidal. For a long time, people have struggled to reconcile this with what appears to be a very different view of God in the New Testament. Again, we need to realize this is *their view* of God then — *their* understanding of what God was asking them to do or what they perceived God was telling them he would do *then*.

In other words, as we read, the things that biblical figures "hear God" asking of them or saying to them have to be filtered through their very different historical context, which is accompanied by a very different understanding of God. If we do not recognize how they understood God in their context and historical epoch, we may find ourselves creating all sorts of inappropriate applications stemming from our desire to "obey the Bible." I think we are in real danger if we assume that every single one of these snapshots of people interacting with God is an accurate view of the God we serve today.

I am not arguing that God is evolving; I am suggesting that our view of God over time changes and that these changes are often deeply tied to cultural and epochal contexts of the people in the stories. Of course, the context of the writers' worldviews themselves can further complicate matters. Such things as their mental models, social contexts, and cultural milieus would all have to be taken into consideration.

Where did we get the idea that Abraham's Bronze Age view of God was one we needed to adopt? Or that the perception of God as sending an evil spirit (Judges 9:23) is accurate, even helpful, in our understanding of God in the twenty-first century? I do realize in that era and epoch the gods were seen as sending evil spirits, but this does not mean the people of that day had an accurate view of God. Nor does the idea that we have an inspired biblical text nullify, mute, or neutralize the historical era in which they lived. Inspiration does not take a historically conditioned or situated text and make the views of God and the world somehow up-to-date and in sync with modern or even postmodern sensibilities.

Maybe using the changing view of the world and cosmology is a good and less volatile example. We do not think Joshua's praying for the sun to stand still several thousand years ago makes an earth-centered (geocentric) view of the universe correct because our Bible is inspired. On the contrary, we consider that the cosmology of the day was geocentric and that Joshua had no other framework in which to operate. I am suggesting that the issue of understanding God is identical. Historical era will determine how the biblical characters, authors, and we today think about all of these things. Inspiration does not diminish or neutralize historical location.

I think it is fair to say that inspiration does not ensure every view of God presented in the Bible is the correct, accurate, or best view. I assume that God will not ask me in a dream to kill my firstborn son—but I don't live in the Bronze Age. While it would never dawn on me that God might request this of me, I think we can assume it did not seem like an off-the-map request in Abraham's mind. We pick up any ancient document with the full understanding of the huge time gap between us — our culture, our worldview — and those we are reading about. It doesn't matter if we are reading fourth-century BC Aristotle on metaphysics, first-century AD Ptolemy on the geocentric view of the universe, or sixteenth-century Shakespearean literature. Their worldviews, understanding of life, values, cultural mores, and social systems will reflect their historical and geographical location. And what we say of these ancient documents is also true of the Bible. Inspiration in no way erases or eases any of these specificities.

What does inspiration do then? What does it ensure? And what is unique about Scripture? The passage where the Bible declares it is inspired — 2 Timothy 3:16 — simply says the inspired text is useful for teaching, rebuking, correcting, and training in righteousness so that we might be thoroughly equipped for good works. Inspiration means this text has been "spirited" to shape a human life. But what this text does not say is *how* the inspired text is to shape our lives. Does that shaping come from picking and choosing one-liners we will try to align ourselves with? Or is there something larger in play as to how this inspired text shapes and exercises authority in a human life?

Whether we are talking about child sacrifice or human slavery — which still goes on in overt and covert ways in various parts of the world — concubines or eating shellfish, it makes sense to dismiss these as passé due to the evolving of culture through and then past these conventions that now, decades, centuries, or millennia later, are seen as primitive, unspiritual, or illegal, or as violations of human civil rights.

Don't these examples illustrate something important to grasp in the grand scheme of approaching the Bible? Aren't every people group, every community of faith, every New Testament church (Ephesus, for instance) referred to in the Bible bound to their historic location, just as we see in, say, the Abraham story? Isn't all of the New Testament a snapshot in time of a particular people with a certain set of questions and a certain understanding of God as they work out their relationships with each other and God in their own unique context? Don't they have their way of meaning making? Don't they have a unique way of answering their questions in their context with their unique knowledge in that time period? And won't what they think of God/gods and how they operate affect what they "hear"—what they think is being asked of them and said to them?

When did we come to think that any of the Bible's injunctions, principles, or propositions were to be directly applied to ourselves? Why did I think that by meditating on the Book of the Law day and night, a la Joshua 1:8, I would be successful in whatever I do? Those words weren't written to me, any more than the statement to Noah to build a football field–sized boat was written to me. The operative phrase here is *directly applied*. Neither of those phrases or injunctions was written to Ron Martoia in the twenty-first century in the Midwestern United States.

We often read and apply the Bible as though it is written directly to us. However, even a bygone era's most obvious practices that are no longer in effect we would consider ludicrous to apply. Just how are we determining what is instantly applicable and what isn't? I assure you that even members of the academy are trying to figure out how to deal with this pick-and-choose dilemma.

A SHRINKING ARSENAL

As the guiding question of what is timeless and what is not stays front and center, an enormous problem is encroaching. If the Bible, due to its being written over a long period of time, shows definite shifts in values due to social evolution — such as concubines to no concubines, child sacrifice to no sacrifice — then aren't we in grave danger of having a shrinking arsenal of principles to draw from? Does the shift in our understanding of what is acceptable and not acceptable, what is expected and not expected, suggest that the Bible is teaching us that values change?

Is homosexuality, for instance, now acceptable because our culture has changed? Until quite recently, the conservative evangelical church held a cut-and-dried position on the timeless truths Paul writes about in Romans 1:18 – 32. Not anymore. What was once so obvious and timeless is now a matter of serious scholarly and spirited conversation about how much of what Paul said was cultural and illustrative teaching and how much was timeless truth for the ages.[4]

What do we do about tongues and interpretation? Spontaneity in the church service was clearly a value in Corinth. What about in our churches? Certain injunctions just seem easier to say it was "for them back there" than others.

If our goal is to uncover what is timeless and what is not — regardless of what kind of hermeneutics and Bible study method we use — then I think we are in deep trouble. These categories of *timeless* and *cultural* were not in the minds of the biblical writers. They were writing purely occasional letters and documents they may never have imagined would be read by future generations, let alone be the rule book for millennia to come.

Think about how this relates to those passages about the end of the world (what we earlier called eschatology). We read Matthew 24 and Mark 13 as though they were written directly to us. We ignore Jesus' comment that his predictions would happen within the generation of those he was talking to (Matthew 23:36; 24:34), that the things he was speaking of would come to pass before the disciples finished going through the towns of Israel preaching a message of repentance and judgment (Matthew 10:23). We assume these words of Jesus were written to us because they are timeless, and we barely consider the bearing they had on those to whom they were originally written.

We read the glorious conclusion to Paul's prayer in Ephesians 1 and think that Jesus' exaltation above all powers is about how he has overcome cancer, diabetes, lupus, and Alzheimer's. But the context had some definite cultural tones. We have specific background material in Acts 19 about the church at Ephesus. The city of Ephesus had a huge appeal to the surrounding world as a hotbed of occult spiritual activity because it housed the huge statue and temple of Artemis, considered one of the Seven Wonders of the Ancient World.

Think about living in a city where one of the primary industries was making little idols of Artemis to sell. Consider the huge service industry surrounding the tourist attraction and supporting the religious pilgrimage traffic coming through Ephesus. What would it be like to be a part of a little church plant in the middle of a community that housed something so incredible it came to be known as an ancient wonder of the world—only not to you. You are a Christian. And Jesus isn't second fiddle to Artemis. Just because you are in a small church plant meeting in a house, says Paul, you cannot forget that Jesus is far above every rule and authority. Paul prays that the eyes of your heart may be enlightened and that you will come to grips with the hope to which you are being called and with the amazing inheritance you have in the saints.

What do the typical Ephesus church attendees hear when they read this prayer of Paul? They instantly know what Paul is referring to because they live in a context where people from far and wide come and worship a very different god/goddess—a statue so high it could be seen from miles away. So when Paul uses "far above" language, they get what he is talking about. When he says rules, authorities, powers, and dominions, they instantly know what he is referring to. In this light, is it a fair application to say this passage teaches that Jesus will heal your cancer because he is seated above cancer and the name of Jesus is above the name of cancer?

THE BIBLE AS A CHILTON MANUAL

"The Bible isn't a timeless Chilton Manual, Ron; it just isn't." Kevin and I were having a conversation about how we use the Bible.

While my dad wasn't a wrenchhead, he surely was 100 percent an automotive engineer, so I had heard of a Chilton Manual. Let's say you have a 1964 Corvette that needs some work done on it. Where are you going to get a '64 manual to guide you? Chilton is your best bet. They provide manuals for every year, model, and make of car you can come up with.

But then, how much help would a '64 Corvette manual be for doing engine work on a 2009 Corvette? I am a car idiot. I know when to change the oil, how to change a flat, and how to put on new windshield wiper blades—and that represents most of my car know-how. But I will venture a guess that the 1964 manual will be virtually useless for your 2009 engine work. A lot of changes have taken place in the Corvette in the last thirty-five years. You could try to find some diagrams in the manual that look close to the engine block you have in front of you, and no doubt you will find rough similarities; but that is probably all the crossover you will find.

The point is, we tend to use the Bible with a lack of awareness that there is a specific year, model, and make of community about whom and to whom the documents are written. So as we read the document, we look for something that connects with us—whatever looks like it could make the jump into our culture and time period—and grab it and run.

So if we cannot read and apply the Bible as though it is written directly to us, what other options do we have?

NEW METAPHORS FOR THE SHIFT

Reading Classics and Playing Jazz

IF THE BIBLE is useful for teaching us, then *how* is its truth to be applied? How are we to unearth the truth that is to be applied? It is true that Abraham climbed a mountain to sacrifice Isaac; it is true that Jonah was swallowed by a great fish; it is true that Malachi told the Israelites they had to stop robbing God and offer the entire tithe. All these are true statements. Are these supposed to apply to us in some way? Are these truths the things that we are to take and recontextualize for shaping our lives today? Or is there something else going on in the Bible? Is the historical narrative of the Bible asking of us something more intimate, powerful, and overarching? What are some possible alternative metaphors?

I have been toying around with the idea of the Bible as a classic for some time now, and the metaphor is as instructive as it is fruitful.[1] Just saying the word *classic* will evoke in us certain expectations and ways of reading. Whatever we expect to find will largely guide what we see. Remember our quantum mechanics insight? When we come to the Bible to read it as a doctrinal book, we find doctrines; when we approach it as the rule book for life, we find rules and principles. But what happens when we come to the text to read it as a classic? How will doing so change what we read for and therefore what we see?

A text reaches "classic" status as, over a period of time, it is "passed on." *Moby Dick, The Brothers Karamazov,* and *Hamlet* are all classics that when originally written were merely an author's attempt to tell a great story. These particular volumes caught on—and were passed on for generations. I remember learning about this in my first exposure to classics when I was in grade school and participated in the Great Books Program. I was placed in a "small group" in which we read great literature and then had a discussion about it with peers that was facilitated by an adult mentor.

Mortimer Adler founded the Great Books Program and promoted the concept of reading the greatest classics that contained the 102 great ideas of Western Civilization (see *www.thegreatideas. org*). Adler felt that these ideas were seminal shaping influences—the foundation of what he called a "truly liberal arts" education—and he wanted to see as many people as possible, as early in life as possible, engage these books.

How does a classic achieve "classic" status? There is no committee voting on a list of books to determine which ones receive the coveted label. Classic status happens over time. Something like this occurs: You read a good book and suggest it to a friend—and within a year or two, no one remembers the book. But what happens when you read a book and a whole bunch of other people read the book because the book's plot and story line are compelling? The characters who face life's dilemmas and grow in the light of their challenges have a staying power or stamina that is engaging and attractive. The book has marked you and is valued by you.

Let's say a huge number of those who read it recommend the book to friends and feel as though their kids need to read it too. Maybe it achieves national bestseller status. As the kids become adults, maybe they decide to read the book to their kids too. And soon generation after generation read it because of its forming and shaping influence. Before you know it, a book's enduring quality has been identified because it has been around for several generations—or even centuries or millennia. Greek mythology, Homer, Shakespeare, Dickens all earned "classics" status for their writings.

Earlier I mentioned that Mrs. M thought *inspired* might be a good adjective to describe the classics we were reading. That isn't *my* point, however. I'm more interested in how the classic is molding or shaping a life. Never once in reading a classic in the Great Books Program or in my training in literature with Mrs. M (and others) was I ever taught that the value of the classic is found in short memorizable sayings I needed to catalog. Nor was I ever instructed to look for "the moral of the story" in the subplots within the overall story line and apply it to my life. The goal was always *broad synthesis*; it never ended at analysis. The power of a classic lays in something grander than short, pithy, repeatable principles. The classics' power is derived from at least two things: the story line complete with character development and plot tension, and the perennial questions the story line raises as a conversation partner for our lives here and now.

The story line has something enduring to say about the human condition and how we navigate the verities of life. The plot has tensions, challenges, and barriers and raises enduring questions about life and the human condition. The characters illustrate fortitude, errors in judgment, relational ineptness, grace, and insight.

All of these resonate with the real-life situations you and I face today. These qualities are true of sixteenth-century Shakespeare or fourth-century BC Sophocles.

The value of reading the classic is in the broad sweep of interaction with the plot and story line, not in specific repeatable maxims extracted from the text. The goal in reading isn't to find insightful quotes on the lips of the characters, which are memorized and applied at the right moment in life so everything will work out like the plot in the original story. The goal is substantially different.

David Tracy, who has written about viewing the Bible through the metaphor of a classic, is quite clear: when we merely parrot or apply the principles or precepts of any tradition, whether it is the biblical or historical tradition of Christianity, we are being naive, which is dangerous. He says the goal in interpreting the classic is not a repetition of the past *into* the present but a mediation of the two.[2]

When we look at the biblical text in the light of the "classic" metaphor, we see that the interactions of the characters in the biblical story may or may not find parallel situations in our lives. What happened to Jonah hasn't happened to me. His calling was unique and unrepeatable. While this may seem obvious, I'm sure the truth is often lost on us. Why? If Jonah's situation is unique and his circumstances are different from mine (that is the obvious part), then why do I think I should mimic his response or lack of response to God? Tracy suggests there is another way to learn from and apply the content of any classic: we must enter into a conversation with the "subject matter" of the text.

This is a slightly slippery term requiring explanation. Tracy says that "subject matter" is composed of the key questions the classic raises. These questions are first composed of the challenges, problems, barriers, relationships, evil, and the like raised in the narrative and plot of the story. Those issues raised in the plot are then interacted with, mulled over, bantered about in the interactions of the plot's characters. Subject matter, then, is this interacting complex of plot issues and characters. All classics offer the subject matter for the readers' conversation and consideration.

The notion of *conversation* is the key point. The main point in the classic isn't a specific problem in the text that a specific character responds to. The idea of "subject matter" invites us to converse with something broader, more sweeping, and more winsome; and in doing so, we see what we can learn about our own lives in our own context. In this way the classic has a timeless quality to it—not because there are transferable maxims that stand firm through the ages but because the subject matter provokes revelatory conversation that is life transforming.

Obviously, the outcome of the classic narrative and questions raised in response to the story by the characters may or may not have crossover application in our time. Tracy's point is that they don't need to. The classic's molding influence lives on in our new historical context—now possibly centuries or millennia removed from the original writing—precisely because the questions raised and the interactions with those questions (what Tracy calls the subject matter) create a transformative conversation arena with the reader.

For Tracy those are the values of the classics—both literary and biblical. As we the reader enter into true conversation with the questions, thus giving the classic a longer shelf life, we enter into the transformative work of the classic, into the power of the narrative, into the shaping influence of the author. The influence isn't because we are supposed to reenact, replay, recite, or mimic any of the characters' life choices or responses but because we are asking questions today of some of the classics in a new context, culture, and time.[3]

Using the category of "classic" to describe the Bible and the religious tradition of Christianity in no way denigrates the inspired status of the Scriptures. Rather, I'm attempting to get at the question of *how* the biblical text exercises authority. To recite, replay, or reiterate the biblical tradition *only* is to lose forever the living force of the text. Instead, we must mediate the classic's past subject matter with the current "present" of our lives through a conversation we engage in with the text.[4]

JONAH AS CLASSIC—AT LEAST

Take the book of Jonah as an example of a classic. Whether you think the book is a myth, a historical narrative of actual events, or merely an illustration is secondary to the book's function for the Christian community or for anyone who might read it. The book of Jonah raises questions about what happens when we feel a compelling sense of call by God to do something we are not keen on doing.

What makes the book of Jonah unique or spiritual or Scripture or a classic? I think this is exactly where the idea of classic is so helpful.

The questions raised in the plot are questions that include the "God factor." Not all story lines share this dimension explicitly. Therefore, the "subject matter," to use Tracy's category, includes a divine dimension that has to be considered as we think about the questions raised and the responses and reactions of Jonah. This divine dimension is what, at least in part, makes it Scripture or worthy of our attention or different from other forms of classics.

When it comes to Jonah, we could focus on the minutiae of evangelistic strategy or the preaching content of Jonah's message, both of which I've heard preached as *the* point of the story. I have also heard this narrative held over the heads of Christians numerous times as a warning to evangelize—because if you don't, bad things can happen. As recently as this past week, I heard Jonah appealed to as a warning narrative about what happens when you deny a call to ministry. I have to say all these seem right-hearted but wrongheaded. They are anachronistic, out of time sync, so to speak.

If we really believe all those things about Jonah, do we also believe that a storm—a physical, life-threatening storm that crops up in the proximity of our denial of a "call"—has been placed there by God and that we, too, should throw ourselves into a situation of sure death to get God to stop the storm? These would be wholly legitimate conclusions if we think those other applications are fair. These are the crazy implications of our often-used approach, which only glaringly shows how ready we are to pick what to apply and how equally ready we are to feel free to ignore.

Of course, those who think Jonah is about evangelism typically argue that the Bible is timeless truth and therefore it *is* about prescribing such an idea, and yet I don't know of anyone who is preaching the "throw yourself into a raging sea" application in Jonah 1. This is only one more reason the "timeless truths we must unearth" approach has to be jettisoned.

What if the book of Jonah is more about how we handle liminal experiences? What if Jonah is about what happens as we sense a call from God to move out of our comfort zone into unknown and new terrain? Jonah was being asked to journey to a faraway place to preach to a group of people he wasn't keen to impress, and he decided to run. If we can step back from the text for a moment it is a little easier to see the contours of the story from the vantage point of a classic.

We have been taught and trained to drill down into the text—to analyze verbs and cull historical and geographical details. While this doesn't seem to be a bad idea on the surface, it makes the text primarily the domain of the scholar. But just how necessary is it? We can't plead, "Because it is the inspired word of God." Inspiration is not a licensing of a new or unique approach for muting the Bible's wide span across various epochs of history; it is our admission that we believe God has breathed out the text.

What do we learn from Jonah as we glance at the book from 50,000 feet? I think it is Jonah finding himself in layers of liminality.

- Layer #1: Jonah is called by God to preach to a group of people, and he runs. There is a personal sense of disorientation when a human being clearly hears from God but then denies it. I have experienced it, and I'm sure you have too.

- Layer #2: Jonah hits this layer when he finds himself in a life-threatening storm. The mythical and magical worldview of the sailors with whom Jonah has enlisted leads them to the certain conclusion that this storm is the work of the gods. It doesn't stop there though. They are also convinced that a storm of this magnitude implies someone among them is responsible. Jonah fesses up and urges them to toss him overboard. In this second layer of disequilibrium, he finds himself on the outs with God as well as with the sailors, who unbeknownst to themselves were helping Jonah run.

- Layer #3: This layer is experienced as Jonah moves from the life-threatening storm to the life-consuming fish-swallowing incident. How much more vertigo can one guy take? Jonah is now facing what had to feel like certain death.

These details all occur in the first chapter of a four-chapter book. This isn't the place to give an exhaustive analysis of the book of Jonah. The point is that when we fly higher, some slightly different themes emerge that are relevant, timeless, valuable. Such insights will not be found by looking for strategic, programmatic, or propositional extractions from the book. The reframing I suggest here creates questions raised by the "classic," and these questions open up a conversation space for readers to engage their real-life situations of call, liminality, fleeing, and repercussions. Our conversation with the "subject matter" of Jonah creates a far more powerful, life-shaping narrative than we could find simply by looking for principles and propositions.

And this is precisely the *unique* contribution the Bible makes. The timeless propositions it offers we would all agree on — such as love God, love your neighbor, and be kind to others — are found in the sacred scriptures of most world religions. What is unique in the biblical narrative is, well, the narrative. The sweep of a story line, a story line that invites you and me to reframe our story in the light of a bigger God story, cannot be found any place else. This is something other world religions do not provide — a larger framing, healing narrative into which our smaller stories can be fit, re-understood, and reshaped.

When we investigate further how Jonah fits into the plot structure other classics share, far from finding a diminishing of the power of the book, we realize the unique dimensions and life-shaping themes. The biblical books, such as Jonah, are more than a classic to us, but they are *at the very least* a classic. If we think that, because the Bible is inspired, it cannot function as a classic, we will have to conclude that the biblical writers wrote unique forms of literature that were totally out of step with the conventions of the day, which doesn't seem to be the case. Examining the way in which great narratives of history shape people's lives seems to be getting closer to how stories such as Jonah's are to function.

I find it rather easy to conceive of Jonah as a classic in the ancient world prior to being included in the canon. Someone somewhere had to start passing the book along, finding value in its themes and life-shaping power. As the book was passed on, it became "classic" and then, and only then, did it get consideration for inclusion in a special group of classics called the Bible.

HOW ABOUT JAZZ IMPROV?

The classic may be a helpful category, but it has nothing on the jazz metaphor. I had my first taste of playing jazz when I was in high school. As a trombone player, I played in the jazz band for three of my four years. It is a complex art form, one I understood far better than I was able to actually execute. In all honesty, I never really did it well, no matter how hard I tried.

I remember the first time I had to improv. Sounds so cool, so tough, so accomplished, but to pull it off takes real talent. Improvisation works only if you know well the piece and the chord structure it is built around. You have to have sound fundamentals concerning basic chords, the notes in those chords, and the creative latitude you can have within that structure. You also have to listen to those you are playing with so you can play off their improv. You aren't merely freelancing as a soloist; you are playing in the context of a "community" of musicians.

When Jim on trumpet improvises his section, a good follow-up trombone improv might echo strains or note sequences Jim created. In this way the improv sections not only reflect waves and countermelodies of the written score but also the ad hoc, on-the-fly created music of those improvising. It is one thing to improv a solo when no one else is going to do one; it is an entirely different thing to be able to improv in community, where the final product of all the improvisations by all the musicians creates a seamless whole.

When we completed a concert, we would talk about how we did at hearing the others in the group and how well we picked up on their themes and the "hard" themes of the score. We were learning how to collaborate and carry on a conversation through our music making. At times we did a great job communicating with each other and the score, even if our "language skills" were basic; at other times it was obvious we either weren't listening well to each other or simply weren't able to execute through our instruments what we heard in our head. You have to hear it before you can play it. Hearing wasn't my problem; it was getting my horn to play what I heard in my head.

The point of improvisation is to build on the score as written by the composer. There is a connection, some sort of umbilical cord to the original, but the improv certainly isn't simply a repetition of the score. Good improv is in keeping with the original but unearths new things within the framework of the original. Some would say we are creating new music beyond the original work of the composer; others describe improv as unlocking the inherent potential of the original. Our goal was immersion in the score of the music so we knew it well, and we also sought connection to those in our jazz group so we could echo, build on, and flow together.

I think this is a great metaphor for our approach to Scripture. The point of Scripture is much like that of a jazz score. For a long time we have recited, repeated, memorized, and attempted to reenact or mimic the score of the Bible. I think our lives in relationship to Scripture are more like the relationship of improvisation to the music score. The goal isn't memorization for the purpose of recitation or repetition. Immersion in the author's "world" is important but not because the goal is repetition. Improv is not a repetitive but a reinterpretive enterprise. The reinterpretation is done in continuity with the score, builds on the score, and can be done only when you have at some level engaged the score. But impro-visation isn't merely repeating the score; to do so is to fall short of bringing the music to life through the horn of your personality.

The Bible is no different. The goal isn't to repeat or recite the Bible. The Bible has to live through the music I am making with my life. The Bible is being reinterpreted for the moment here and now—a reinterpretation that is happening in continuity with the Bible as originally written but may or may not include any of the same responses the characters in the Bible had.

The importance of the jazz metaphor for me includes not only the idea of performance trajectory but the required community dimension of improv. The jazz musician is doing improvisation within the context of a larger community. The jazz ensemble is a trusted cohort. There is an intimacy developed over time that is required for improv to happen effectively. The ensemble has presumably agreed on goals, commitments to the score, musi-cianship, excellence, and the importance of a deep commitment to each other. A built-in support and feedback team is in the mix every time someone enters those personal, solitary moments of the improv world. This is the beautiful dance of improv. I am doing the solo. It is on my shoulders. It will be filtered through my interpreta-tion of the composer's score, my sensitivity to what others before me have done, and my abilities to allow my horn to be an extension of my head and heart. All of these go into what we might term "faith-ful improvisation."

I hope the parallels between the jazz improv musician and the Christ-following Bible reader are becoming clearer. We have been given a score called the Bible. All of us have to think about "performance trajectory" and about approaching the Bible in the context of a larger community we call the church, the "called-out ones." We have to immerse ourselves in the score of the Bible to understand the shape and contour of the main thing the composer is trying to accomplish. Just as we cannot study one or two measures, or even a whole line, of a score and understand what the composer is trying to do, neither can we expect to understand the whole of what God has composed by reading snippets or lines of the Bible. It will take a much more intentional immersion in the sweep of the whole musical piece.

Just as the improv musician is given feedback by others in the group as to how faithfully their improv reflected the composer's score and played off the improv of others in the group, so each Jesus-follower does his or her life improv in the context of a community of people who can give feedback about how the music of their lives sounds and plays in the wider arena of all of life. This Christian community presumably has commitments to the "score," sealed with its intentions to support, encourage, and give feedback to our very best music making. All of this seems tightly parallel with the jazz ensemble.

In some ways, David Tracy's conversation with the "subject matter" of the classic, a conversation that has happened with many people throughout many ages, is similar to the conversation of community in the jazz group or Christian community. Given the high degree of individualism and autonomy in our modern world and often in the church, this community dimension is an important detail we need to emphasize.

We are taught early in our development to read the Bible, the assumption being that we will be interpreting it on our own. While this assumption isn't entirely true, at least theoretically, in practice this is how it typically plays out. We have doctrinal statements, sermons from the pulpit, and correction that can be given when we get off base either theologically or practically; but once we start reading the Bible, we are going to interpret that book through our inherited lenses and largely on our own. The Christian spiritual life project, unfortunately, often isn't so much a jazz ensemble as it is a solo practice session that involves going over the same material time and again. There is little of community speaking into my interpretive ideas, little of history or tradition creating a tried and true boundary within which the life improv can be conducted.

The power of Tracy's classics metaphor is that it reveals the value of the text *established over time*. In the Christian community we call it *tradition*. The value of the jazz metaphor is that it shows how much we need real-time feedback to give and receive from each other. Both metaphors capture the idea that repetition or mimicking of the text or score is not the goal; what is critical is that we build on the text. We are to live it again in a new way and for a new day. Both conversation with subject matter and improv are alive and dynamic. How can we bring the two together?

PART 3

IMPROV-ING THE SCRIPT

Learning to Riff in Community

My journey into seeing the Bible in a totally new way has not been without pain. Being challenged by mentors to reconsider my early Christian upbringing and how it shaped my approach to the Bible has been at times unsettling. When you have firm ideas from which you operate and lenses that you assume are clear, it is hard to make a change. I will be the first to say the chapters in this section represent a proposal of sorts — a suggestion, a possibility, an option — that I hope proves fruitful in moving the conversation forward. In my own journey I have come to realize that new paradigms and lenses will never be explored until the liabilities and intractable problems of the current one become too excruciating to live with any longer.

A new model is not easy to design; it is certainly not easy to adopt. As I've talked about these issues in conference settings and churches all over the world, people instantly resonate with the interpretive problems we face. I know of few people in the Christian community who at some level don't feel these inconsistencies at the visceral level, even if they haven't thought them through intellectually.

In the remaining pages of this book I want to take a stab at popular-izing a metaphor that has come from one of the brilliant scholarly minds of our time and that I believe helps resolve many of the conundrums our current model has generated. It also highlights the role of com-munity, something woefully absent from most of our biblical reading exercises. A new paradigm, while answering many questions that have been put on the shelf for future examination, also raise new questions that over time have to be wrestled with. With the understanding that both of these dynamics are present, let's look at the Shakespearean drama as metaphor.

ELEVEN

CHAPTER

THE DRAMA SCRIPT

Blending the Story Line of the Classic with Jazz Community

MY FIRST EXPOSURE to the idea of drama as a metaphor for reading the Bible came through an article I read years ago that continues to percolate in my mind.[1] Two things stuck with me. First, the Bible isn't really the authority; it is the God the Bible points to who has authority. Any authority or life-shaping power of the biblical text comes from the God who is behind the words. Second, the Bible therefore doesn't exercise authority through propositions but through something more elegant, subversive, and powerful.

N. T. Wright uses the metaphor of story, and specifically a play/drama in which a story is enacted, to develop these points.

Suppose a Shakespearean play of five acts has been written. The play is compelling and lively and has depth of character development and a plot and story line that beg to be staged. There is only one problem: the fifth act of this five-part play has been lost. To have this play performed, we have a couple options. First, we could give the four acts to gifted Shakespearean scholars and commission them to write a fifth act, which would complete the truncated play. The second option, using a more organic, "living" approach, hands the first four acts to some gifted Shakespearean actors, with the goal that these actors immerse themselves in the script of the first four acts and then perform the play *improvising* the fifth act.

Wright anticipates what may happen if we were to take this approach:

> Consider the result. The first four acts, existing as they did, would be the undoubted "authority" for the task in hand. That is, anyone could properly object to the new improvisation on the grounds that this or that character was now behaving inconsistently, or that this or that sub-plot or theme, adumbrated earlier, had not reached its proper resolution. This "authority" of the first four acts would not consist in an implicit command that the actors should repeat the earlier parts of the play over and over again. It would consist in the fact of an as yet unfinished drama, which contained its own impetus, its own forward movement, which demanded to be concluded in the proper manner but which required of the actors a responsible entering in to the story as it stood, in order first to understand how the threads could appropriately be drawn together, and then to put that understanding into effect by speaking and acting with both *innovation* and *consistency*.[2]

Wright goes on to suggest some possible parallels between the four acts and four major sections/themes of Scripture. The four acts he suggests are creation, the fall, the life and history of Israel, and the life and ministry of Jesus. The fifth act would be comprised of two scenes: *the New Testament*, which gives hints of how the whole drama is to conclude (Romans 8 and 1 Corinthians 15 are good examples), and *the improvisation of the church* in living out the script of the drama.

Beyond this quick hint of how he would spin out this metaphor, we have nothing more from Wright. He does state clearly, however, that it is "inappropriate [for the church] simply to repeat verbatim passages from earlier sections" of Scripture.[3] His observation that the church often does this leads him to suggest that it ought to improv the fifth act.

Wright's Shakespearean drama metaphor is worth pursuing. A drama image values the content of the script as a guiding force for all that is done in the fifth act of the play. The actors will have to immerse themselves in the script, but they will do so for a purpose quite different from what I was taught growing up, different from what I did in the Study in high school, and different from what I taught during nearly twenty years in ministry. Immersion in the script will not be for finding analogues to my current experience so I can execute commands in the text given to those characters with the hope that my outcome will be like theirs. The point of script immersion—knowing the Bible thoroughly—is to understand the overarching, life-shaping, improv-informing story line. We will want to understand the story of stories, their key questions, and the ways in which those questions of life were answered.

The Bible, like all scripts, has a narrative logic, a message being communicated in the whole. I am presupposing something about the whole of the biblical script. The sixty-six various books that were finally put together within the two leather covers of the volume we call the Bible have a cohesive story. They haven't been haphazardly selected and randomly compiled. Our understanding of canon and inspiration is the basis for what we expect is a cohesive story and message. The implications of this narrative consistency mean we have to make sense of the whole meta-story and not just the individual stories. We are interested in the sweeping narrative, the story of stories, and how it helps frame the smaller individual stories.

Part of our job is to wrestle with and reflect on what we as a community of Jesus-followers think the script says. How were the biblical characters wrestling with what it meant to be a people of God then and there? Without understanding the overarching narrative logic and flow, we are in danger of reducing the biblical narrative to a compilation of disconnected individual stories, which is, in fact, the way many of us have been taught to read the Bible. In Sunday school at my old Presbyterian church, we would skip around the Old and New Testaments from week to week with absolutely no rationale as to why we studied the story of Jacob and Esau this week, the story of the woman at the well the previous week, and a passage from Colossians the following week. What I had modeled throughout my Christian experience is that the Bible is a collection of isolated stories that teach us applicable moral truth. Teaching moral truth is not wrong, but we eventually need to get past the "moral of the children's story" approach and learn the sweep of the whole.

If we dissect the Bible to a compilation of various stories for which we are looking for applicable morals, how is the Christian Scripture any different from the Buddhist, Islamic, or Hindu scriptures? They have stories too—stories that can mirror down the line the full range of virtues that a moral-of-the-story approach produces. Love others, help the less fortunate, follow the Golden Rule, nurture basic character traits, live with love and joy rather than hate and anxiety—these and a catalog list of more are common in the scriptures of every major religion. The distinctives aren't in the details. The uniqueness of the Christian Scripture is the overarching drama from beginning to end—and the fact that we have been invited into the drama.

In the text of the Bible we have not only the drama of God's interaction with the world in and through Jesus but also God's address to future actors as they seek to play a role in the unfolding drama in the world.[4] We cannot atomize the whole into bite-sized, memorable portions and expect to understand the narrative contours well enough to improvise a conclusion in continuity with the whole. Script immersion is for the purpose of catching a glimpse of the whole. Bible reading is for the purpose of identifying macro themes and micro subthemes, understanding plot crescendo and barriers to resolution, and becoming aware of the whole host of things that accompany great drama writing.

How do we come to understand the wide sweep of the narrative? I know of no other way except *conversation*. Whether we are talking about conversation with the "subject matter" of the classic, the jazz ensemble discussing the score and goal of the composer before improvising, or an acting guild doing a script read-through to get a feel for the whole, all of these require conversation with a larger community; none of this can be done in isolation. Community conversation is the only way to avoid privatized, idiosyncratic, crazy, and just plain wrong readings of the whole. Like any great drama, the biblical script is complex and layered.

You can't read Dostoyevsky one time, state the theme, and think you have captured it. There will likely be more to think about, others whom you will want to listen to, and ways of expressing the sweeping drama that you may want to adopt or integrate as you hear them articulated by fellow readers. You may even find it helpful to consult a Dostoyevsky expert who has spent years reading his work to discern his or her take on the story. Reading

Dostoyevsky in a small group can be part of a fruitful and fascinating conversation.

The need for this kind of communication in our biblical reading is no different. We may think this is what Bible study is for, and I agree. But the way we have been taught to do Bible study and the way it has been modeled for us often push us to look at little pieces of the whole and rarely discuss or even read for big-picture themes. We need both the historical and our contemporary community as conversation partners if we hope to improv the fifth act.

Far from extracting timeless truth, our holistic reading is intended to improvise in continuity with the sweep of the drama. This is the genius of the "fifth act" metaphor. The Shakespearean actors have to master the script. They have to be intimate with the story line and subplots. Any faithful improvising of the final act will have to be on the same trajectory of the script, picking up on the hints and clues provided as to how the drama will end.

What is *faithful trajectory*? Here "jazz ensemble" meets "classics conversation." The only way we can know if our understanding of the drama is askew is to be in a community of other actors who can help reflect back to us what they are seeing come out of our lives. There is nothing new in this idea of *community accountability*; but we may need to reconsider what accountability means as we read text in community. Certainly we cannot understand the sweep of the whole of the biblical drama if we don't understand the overarching theme, story line, shape, or contour of the entire book.

The jazz ensemble community is an apt metaphor here because it provides the two-pronged feedback we need in order to grow in understanding: *score interpretation* (Do we as musicians get the composer's goals, quirks, style?), and *improv feedback* (How did we do in faithfully improvising the score?). Both are important functions of the community. While I think Christians can do more of both, I fear we rarely do much of the former.

A word about climax and ending. In this metaphor we, the church, are the actors improvising the fifth act. There is a good chance, of course, that we will not be the ones actually concluding the play. So we live between scene 1 and the last scene of the fifth act. We know a little bit about the final scene but absolutely nothing about the duration of the fifth act. What this means for how we improv will be the subject of the next chapters.

IMMERSING IN THE FIRST FOUR ACTS

Reading the Bible Again for the First Time

THE IDEA OF God leaving us a four-act drama script into which he has invited us to read and then participate is a winsome model that left me feeling exhilarated and motivated when I first heard about it.

If we are going to engage the first four acts, we will have to quit seeking certainty and control. Rather than looking to the Bible to sort everything out, lock down the way things are and should be, and give us a predictable, tamed, and consistent existence on the planet as we await eternal life, we can embrace Bible reading as a stepping-stone to a whole new life. The life Jesus brought to this earth courses with the power of streams and rivers; it brings sight where there is blindness and freedom where there are shackles. The predictable orderly deal? It just isn't there.

The biblical text has example after example showing us that everyday life is the theater of God's activity, sometimes in quietly mundane ways, sometimes in disruptively dramatic ways. Adam and Eve were to experience meaning and a visceral connection to the earth in gardening. Abraham was minding his own business when God interrupted his life and led him on a journey for which he had no MapQuested route or Googled destination. When you begin reading the biblical narrative, one of the first impressions that jumps off the page is that the biblical characters are average, typical, and pedestrian. Yet in the midst of their normal everyday rhythm God comes to them and is at work in and around them. Your average day — my average day — is the theater of God's activity.

The drama script of the text introduces us to an untamed God and to a world where the boundaries and borders we thought existed dissolve; it reveals a narrative that surprises, jostles, grips, and grinds on us. The characters are vulgar, alarming, and often downright wicked and wrong. What else can you say about a story such as the one in Genesis 19 where Lot offers his two virgin daughters for the men outside who would like to have sex with the male guests under his roof? Does Lot need his head examined? How do we explain the abrupt and disquieting picture of a God who sends evil spirits to torment people (see Judges 9; 1 Samuel 16; 18, for example).

The Bible is more real than certain. Then again, this is the nature of real drama scripts. They are arresting, upsetting, and inexplicable. The point isn't static stability. When reading this drama, it is hard not to see life as unruly, unfair, and unpredictable, teeming with surprises and aliveness. The kind of life Jesus said he came to bring is *perissos* life, over-the-top wholeness and fullness.* Our methods of study work against this sense of mystery and paradox by attempting to codify, categorize, apprehend, and

---

*_Perissos_ is the Greek word often translated "abundant," "complete," or "overflowing" (see John 10:10).

certify. They work against the idea of a God who cannot be neatly boxed into the categories of systematic theology.

A living, life-sized—no, God-sized—universe complete with complexity and ambiguity isn't what we would choose in today's chaotic and uncertain world. But then again, maybe that is why the drama script we have been given is exactly the way it is. Try as we might to tame it, the text shows us that life really is "two steps forward, three steps back." Brokenness, suffering, emptiness, struggle—these are the things of real life, not the pristine, neat, and tidy endings of made-for-TV movies. As long as we search for the orderly, predictable God of the Newtonian cause-and-effect world, we will hang on to our distinctively modern God, who is impotent to break out of the machine world we have created. God is bigger and more mysterious than all of that. The drama script we have been given testifies to the messiness of real life.

The grand sweeping narrative has a significant message of hope worth noticing. In the midst of all the mess, God doesn't wince with surprise. *He is present*—fully present. The larger message frame for the drama isn't about how to control and manipulate the laws of life and the God who enforces them. The larger framing story is one of *God's presence* in the midst of all this crazy chaos we call life. This is why Jesus was to be called Immanuel, which means "God with us"—not "God fix us."

I hope I've made a beginning at helping you feel, hear, and see the "something different" I started to feel a few years ago, which pushed me to entertain thinking something different. What was happening in me was a stage-of-faith shift. As my view of the Bible was changing, my view of God couldn't help but change. Or was it the other way around? I can't tell which came first because they were happening simultaneously.

Many of us have been tempted to downplay the affective, emotional, bodily side of our knowing. The truth is, our emotions play a crucial role in how we come to know and an even more important role in how we come to act. And acting is all about what it means to improvise the fifth act. Immersing ourselves in the broad sweeping narrative with suspended judgment is the place we must begin. If this is a drama script, I must allow it to speak to and shape my emotions and thoughts; without this shaping, improvising on the themes will be impossible.

Earlier in the book, I talked a lot about our lenses. Let me return to that topic and tie it to the idea of suspending judgment.

I *THINK* I SEE

One of the most important lessons I've had to learn in the last several years is about my own ability and inability to see, which is a statement about my reading. The late Daniel Boorstin, former Librarian of Congress and author of the three-volume series of intellectual history — *The Discoverers* (1983), *The Creators* (1992), and *The Seekers* (1998) — wrote, "The great obstacle to discovering the shape of the earth, the continents, and the oceans was not ignorance but the illusion of knowledge."[1]

Boorstin, in looking at hundreds of incredible discoveries, goes to great lengths to illustrate that insatiable curiosity, the beginner's mind, unending questions, and holding loosely to previous discoveries in case something better comes along were always the marks of the great thinkers, explorers, and creators throughout human history. I cannot tell you how often I have pondered this quote in relationship to my own life, to what I think about God and the Bible, and to what I think about ministry.

Living under "the illusion of knowledge" applies to my life and ministry, though I hope less now than it did for the first twelve to fifteen years of ministry. We live under the illusion that we know most of it, if not all of it. We know about God and the Bible, and about how to tell people how to live. We know how to help people, fix people, coach people, counsel people — and all because we live under the illusion of knowledge.

I realize that Boorstin was only capitalizing on what Jesus had already presented and captured in John 9 — another constant companion in my recent journey. If we are to believe Jesus, not many things are more dangerous than people who presume they already see. John takes 41 verses to record the story of one of Jesus' healing miracles.

The opening of the story reads almost like a play on words. Jesus sees a man blind from birth. The response of the disciples is interesting. Their worldview was such that they assumed someone's sin had to have been involved, causing the blindness. Not according to Jesus. The blind man would prove to be a life illustration for the power of God.

What ensues with the onlookers — and with the Pharisees in particular — is interesting. The Pharisees are upset that Jesus has healed on the Sabbath. Disobedient, evil people break Sabbath laws. Jesus must then be disobedient and evil, and therefore any healing this man had received (which was up for question too) couldn't have come from God.

> Jesus said, "For judgment I have come into this world, so that the blind will see and those who see will become blind."
>
> Some Pharisees who were with him heard him say this and asked, "What? Are we blind too?"
>
> Jesus said, "If you were blind, you would not be guilty of sin; but now that you claim you can see, your guilt remains."
>
> JOHN 9:39–41

The Pharisees thought all their theological arguments invalidated the healing work of Jesus—which is what Jesus referred to as *blindness*. He says something even deeper though. The real problem is in our being convinced of our impeccable seeing ability, which is proof we cannot see. Arrogance is proof of blindness.

I have to say I was those Pharisees. I was the certain, cocky, call-the-shots guy who had all the theology screwed down. I was the one who liked to make the conservative/liberal polarities and belittle those who weren't as conservative as I was. I was a modernist Pharisee who was, in reality, quite blind.

We are tapping into one of the big themes in the ministry of Jesus. Seeing, awakeness, and alertness—these are the necessary postures of those who will be able to see the kingdom of God. Blessed are the meek and humble and pure in heart, for they will see God.

How well do we see in the theater of the everyday rhythms? In showering and at breakfast? In chauffeuring kids to school, sports practices, and voice lessons? At the office, in the board meeting? Do we see God? Do we see his hand? Do we see his activity?

Humility marks the journey and the script reader. The script isn't to be mastered; it is to be conversed with. It isn't to be memorized or recited; it is to be internalized to prompt creative improvisation. As you and I embark on a new way of reading and acting the script-ure, we need to do it with a beginner's mind. We need to start with the innocence of a first read, with the wonder of a first listen, with the anticipation of a first glimpse.

New lenses begin to be fitted here. We find out soon enough that we have what experts call "inattentional blindness." Studies suggest that our brains are wired to see only a portion of our visual field when our focus is fixed on something else, especially when we are trained to fix that focus.[2] The research seems to indicate that our perception is determined by our attention. Our attention in turn is determined and shaped by our cognitive processes, our mental models, our maps, our lenses. So when from a very early stage I begin to view the Bible and God in a certain way, any material in the Bible that doesn't fit the view of the Bible and God I hold will remain out of my "field of vision." I will be blind to it due to inattention—trained inattention.

You may have already experienced an aha moment at some point in reading this book. Something in the Bible you have read or heard numerous times may have been quite clearly understood until your attention was drawn to something else—and all of a sudden you say, "Why haven't I ever seen that before?" I can't tell you how many times I've said that to myself—just one indication that no matter how clearly we think we see, we see what we are trained, told, guided, and shaped to see.

READ-THROUGH: A NEW PRACTICE?

If we have been given four acts of a five-part drama and our invitation is to improvise the fifth act, then our need to understand the script is nonnegotiable. We will have to do a read-through—multiple read-throughs. We will have to *do them with others* who can help us come to know if we are seeing and hearing the script in concert with how they read it. And we will have to *enlist the help of experts* who have read it in the past.

A couple of key principles introduced here need to be developed. "Coming to know together" may be a lost art in the area of the Bible. Meg Wheatley, in her warm and engaging book *Turning to One Another*, argues that "human conversation is the most ancient and easiest way to cultivate the conditions of change—personal change, community and organizational change, planetary change. If we can sit together and talk about what's important to us, we begin to come alive. We share what we see, what we feel, and we listen to what others see and feel."[3]

Her thesis in the book is that we can change the world if we learn to listen to each other. I admit I was a bit skeptical about "a love for listening" the first time I encountered it — I suppose because my strong suit was talking. I talk; you listen — now that seemed more my cup of tea. But I had heard Meg Wheatley speak on a couple of occasions, and her demeanor was so compelling and her listening as she interacted with us so deep and persuasive that I realized she modeled what she believed and then put it into print. I have employed her ideas in learning conversations, the classroom, and ongoing learning communities. How this focus on listening can help our script reading is an ongoing topic for our conversation.

And as we read the script in community, we will need to evaluate whether we are reading it in concert with the way experts have read it in the past. If after repeated readings of a Shakespearean play large contours of the story are still vague, misunderstood, or totally missed by us, how will we know? Only by consulting a number of scholars and experts who can help us see the history of how this script has been read — and we can figure there probably won't be wild deviations from that history. In other words, we have a tradition we are committed to *respecting* and also *listening to*. We have a long history of experts, called theologians, who have spent their lives reading the script, and we cannot ignore their insights as we engage in the process of coming to know together.

A new frame for approaching the Bible as a dramatic script and seeing life as participatory theater changes how we are reading, what we are looking for, and therefore what we are able to see. Inattentional blindness is challenged by new lenses. Reading for "rules to live by" (the owner's manual for life) suddenly feels thin and superficial in light of the dynamic interplay of dramatic theater. A change in metaphors indeed changes what we can hear and see.

One of the first things we will notice as we read a drama as a script is an unfolding story that has characters who are moving the story. We will search for as full an understanding as possible of these characters and the roles they are playing in the drama. We will be careful to not identify with these characters until we understand what the main contours of the story are, lest we get too immersed in the character before we understand the plot. This is an important observation that I was unable to engage in my early experience. The first questions I asked in the Study in high school were these: How does this apply to me? How can this make my life work better? What is God telling me to do?

Now as I read the script and help others do a read-through, I refrain from identifying with characters and asking myself, "What did they hear from the behind-the-scenes God they are interacting with in this story? Should I listen and respond in the same way?" These questions don't even enter the mind of the one doing a script read-through. They are good questions, but they are premature questions that deal with implications. The first eyes we want to bring to our reading will help us see and uncover the contours of the story line and plot and how the key characters interact, form, deform, and reform themes and subthemes. Before we can get to the implications for my acting and my life, I have to understand this broader sweep first.

It's crucial that we understand this broad sweeping story in order to experience the deepest sort of life change this drama script can provide. The primary invitation God makes to us—and this is what I think we call *conversion*—is to swap the story line we are living, with all its distortions, consumeristic tendencies, and

American Dream overtones, for God's story line, which brings a sense of wholeness and wellness and the awareness of his presence even in the messes of life. We cannot experience deep conversion and the healing and restoration of our life story unless we are clear about the shape and contours of the story into which we are being invited. Of course, this has huge implications not only for our individual life but for the sermons we preach in our churches, for the thinking we do about conversion, and for the practices we engage in as a community of faith.

THE ROLE OF THE "ACTING COMMUNITY"

Designing Creative Conversation Space

OUR ALONENESS AS individuals, even when we are surrounded by neighbors, work colleagues, and "church folk," betrays our lack of connectedness with others, which in turn makes it hard to come to know together. The very idea of having to improvise the fifth act means we have to do it *together*. We see an enormous craving for togetherness in our world and in the church, but I'm not sure we always know how to do togetherness in productive ways.

Community in the church often devolves into control mechanisms for who is out and who is in, or pseudo-accountability that ends up being more about drawing behavior boundaries than doing life together. Of course, these two actions aren't mutually exclusive, but they are different from coming to know together the script we are supposed to be improvising together on the stage we call *today*.

How does this work? My guess is we need to begin by engaging new practices of script read-through. One of the new practices, at least new to me, in the last several years is doing corporate reading of large blocks of Scripture aloud and discussing what people hear.

I have never forgotten the question posed in my first "how to study the Bible" class with Dr. Arden Autry: "Can we agree that the context is a whole book and that it is up to you to read entire books of the Bible in one sitting so you can hear the author's rhythm, cadence, and voice?" I have tried over and over again to reiterate this principle to those with whom I have journeyed over the years. I cannot overstate the value. "Read the Bible in a year" programs set up a way to read sequentially through entire books in sections of three to four chapters a day. For many people this is their first time reading through the whole Bible, and it is often the first time reading a whole book sequentially.

When was the last time you went to a gathering of any sort and read the Bible aloud for at least thirty minutes—not picking and choosing what you want, but reading a sequential section (nine chapters in Jeremiah, for example) and then taking what you have heard read aloud and melding it with previous readings in Jeremiah to understand the sweep of what is going on in that book? Among Christians, this practice is far too infrequent and in some cases nonexistent.

This is an interesting exercise because it engages us in a pre-Gutenberg listening arena. Up until the time of the printed text—the Bible available to every believer—how did they know the Bible? The same way you and I may have originally heard the stories: through a storyteller when we were little kids. Before the invention of the printing press, this was the only way most adults ever heard the biblical stories.[1]

CREATIVE SPACE FUELED BY BIGGER QUESTIONS

Learning to ask new questions of the script is largely fueled by an answer to the larger overarching question, "Why am I reading this particular script-ure at all?"

What are the reasons Paul wrote his letter to the Colossians? What issues was he addressing? What is the basic thrust of the book of Isaiah or Amos? These aren't questions with which we have much familiarity, and they aren't typically taught about much either. Here is what is at stake. These questions bring us to the subplots of the larger story. These are the stories from which the story of stories is developed. If we have no idea about these little stories, then we will certainly be lost when it comes to the "story of stories" metanarrative.

We must shift our questions. We must *stop* asking questions such as: What principles are hidden in these stories? What am I supposed to pull out, memorize, and then at the appropriate moment apply so everything will work out alright? The "what's in it for Ron?" approach to the Bible was so ingrained in my head from my early formative experiences that it has taken years to break the habit.

On a more academic level, I have also stopped asking what truth in the text is eternal and therefore applicable and what in the text is cultural and therefore not applicable. I have engaged a new set of questions that help me fly at 50,000 feet.

- What does this book tell me about how God shows up in the world and about God's workings with humanity?
- How does the worldview unfolding in this story, which is part of the larger story of stories, create a worldview picture for those in the narrative? (When I use the word *worldview*, I do so along the lines of the teaching in chapter 8.)

- What does this book tell me about God's desire, purpose, and plan for the people of God?
- How does what I am reading converge and diverge from the unfolding bigger story of the whole script-ure in which I'm becoming more and more immersed? What does this contribute to the larger script plot that seems new or unique?
- How can we be the people of God today in our context in a way that would be continuous with the story I am reading?
- How does the worldview in the script translate and shape our improvisation today?
- What are the issues I face in my life today that can be shaped and contoured by reorienting my life around God's larger story?

These are the questions I have been asking and refining for some time now for my own reading and for the groups I serve. These are questions that lead to story reflection, to theological reflection. They help push us to frame the whole of the script without getting lost in the details.

WIKI-SYNTHESIS

As we in the community start asking new questions and reading aloud together large blocks of Scripture, conversation becomes immensely valuable. For some people, this will be the first time they have ever read an entire Bible book all the way through. Do some informal surveying. You'll discover that because we have modeled an eclectic, pick-and-choose Bible roulette approach to Scripture, few people have heard an entire book read aloud in one or two sittings. (If Isaiah is on the docket, we would need several meetings to cover all of it.)

After a large block read-through, we invite people to articulate what they heard as we ask them questions about the story line, the plot, and the actions of key characters. This is a sort of wiki-synthesis of the narrative—an open-source, community-developed understanding of the narrative. Everybody gets to contribute to a larger work in progress that is edited on the fly and revisited many times as this durable, testable, and open-ended discussion gains steam.

A wiki-synthesis exercise ought to be a primary practice in the church today. We have given people the atomized, dissected, broken-apart version of the biblical narrative but haven't done as well in helping them capture the big picture. This requires pastors to practice a different sort of skill. Instead of being the shamans and dispensers of gnostic truth—"the stuff only I can learn because I have the tools and you don't"—we become reading facilitators.

How many times have you heard or have you said, "Wow, if I have to do all that background work or know those ancient customs or study those Greek words to get this stuff, I am fresh out of luck"? I hear it all the time. In our efforts to help people understand the text, we discourage them from *reading* the text.[2]

The gift of teaching in the church should *support* our facilitation of the drama read-through, not displace it. As facilitators, we help people discover; we help them come to learn together. For many of us who occupy pastoral positions, we like the sage-on-stage adrenalin rush. We get to be the in-the-know person. We get to be the expert. But that is a bit too much ego if we want to improv in the context of community. Instead, we need gifted teachers to play the role of *master story connector*. We need to have teachers who understand the sweep of the biblical story, facilitate conversation around that story, and then help people connect their stories to the script-ure drama, helping them see how the future of their story will be shaped by that intersection.

The role of the pastor can be to broker the historical communities' reading of the drama. They can provide the resources of what current drama script-ure reading experts are saying these days (read, theologians) and what historically our tradition has understood. Pastors provide context and create containers for community but move out of the mythic role of walking answer manuals. Pastors also have to know how to model and facilitate genuine dialogue.

DIALOGUE: A KEY TO CREATIVE CONVERSATION

If we want to come to know together, we must facilitate the *how* of knowing together. In the church we must be masters of the art of dialogue and help each other learn the art. A church or small group where real dialogue exists will be an exciting place of deep growth and profound understanding that fuels life change. Only out of a context of dialogue can we come to a durable and shared understanding of God's story for us here and now, and only then can we head into improvising and bringing that story into reality today.

The English word *dialogue* comes from two Greek words—*dia* ("through") and *logos* ("word"). Dialogue has to do with finding shared meaning through words. As we come together to read aloud or to converse about the script we have previously read alone, we need to design a creative space where ways of finding shared meaning exist.

This is a dramatically different model from that of the expert on stage dispensing *a* view or, worse yet, *the* view. The church should be leading the way in this art of thinking and knowing together. Who should be modeling the way on how to listen well and deeply? Who better than the church to be patient and suspend judgment and learn how to hear other viewpoints?

The basic idea in dialogue is that we learn to listen from a new and different place. Most of us have a downloading approach to listening. When we hear something, we download it into familiar cubbyholes in our mental model and categorize it. If we don't have cubbies established to house the material, we assume the material is either superfluous or wrong, and so we dismiss it. All of this is automatic and relatively hidden from our awareness. Dialogue shifts the location of listening from inside my models to somebody else's point of view. How does this actually work and how do we engender it?

The first step is *suspending judgment*. We put on hold the certainty we have about our viewpoint and allow others the airspace to voice their understanding. Suspending judgment doesn't mean we stop thinking. We listen with an open mind to other points of view because only by carefully entering into the world of the other can we begin to really hear them. We want to hear them because we realize we don't have all the truth. We don't have the whole story line figured out, and we haven't mastered the script in all its complexities. We come in an attitude of openness, as ready to listen as to give voice. We suspend judgment, realizing that we are participating in a conversation, in a wiki-synthesis project.

The second step in dialogue is *redirection*. When I hear something I don't understand, agree with, or have cubbyholes for in my mental model, instead of going inside myself to begin crafting my rebuttal and pointing out why the speaker is all wrong, I redirect my attention to him and seek to crawl into his thinking. I may pose a clarifying question, I may reflect back what I hear him saying, but I direct my attention toward him instead of doing the reflexively natural thing of crafting my "more intelligent" response.

Can you recall the last time you really listened to someone and discovered she had a reason for believing what she was spouting and had as much heart and emotion invested in her point of view as you did? Do you remember what happened? Something in you shifted. You moved from a place of needing to assert your point or correct her point to a place of broadness, a place of understanding, a place in which you were standing with her to hear and understand her instead of apart from her, over and above her. We have all experienced this in some way. When this shift happens, we are changing the location of our listening.

I like to think of corporate dialogue as a spiritual discipline. Simply read a block of Scripture together and then discuss it. If you have never done this, you will be surprised at how powerful it is. You will be blown away at the insights that come from around the room. The great thing about this? You don't need anything but a few people and a Bible. I have seen this work well with fifteen to twenty people, but more or less works fine. I have done it with up to sixty people.

People ask me, "How long does it take to get through the Bible this way?" I always chuckle at the question. It is like asking how long it will take to end up with $20 worth of change in a piggy bank. The answer is the same in both cases: it depends on how much you cover and how often you do it.

Speed isn't the goal, though I understand why we ask this question. If we simply start reading big blocks of Scripture and move away from the "a verse a day keeps the doctor away" approach, we will move well down the road to new understandings. We need to be reminded that learning the script, immersing in the script, is a lifelong project. Resources for learning dialogue abound.[3]

Having been in several learning communities where we have worked for months on the principles of dialogue and how to apply them to a deeper understanding of God's drama as revealed in the script-ure, I can tell you that something almost magical happens. We come to realize how much of our defensiveness about our positions, understandings, and thoughts about the Bible is unnecessary. Somewhere along the line in our learning we determined we had *the* right answer and therefore had to make this right answer known. Only when I have dropped my defensiveness can I learn from someone whose position is quite different from mine.

As I have learned to really listen, I have moved from pretending to listen to allowing the empathy shift to happen. In those moments I sense greater integrity and integration. What I am portraying—that I am listening to them—I am *actually doing*. I have to point this out because sometimes when I am listening to people, I look fully engaged, nodding my head, making eye contact, humming the "uhhh-huhhhhhh," but the whole time I am really talking to myself: "He just doesn't get it. Isn't this saying of Jesus so stinkin' obvious. Let him talk, Ron, and then help him see where he has it wrong." When I lay that self-conversation down, something inside me happens.

"I'M NOT SURE I GET IT. CAN YOU HELP ME?"

Once we learn to listen from a different place and the listening shift happens, there is a third thing that can emerge in a group. When we come with genuine listening and openness, we enter a creative space where 1 + 1 = 3 or even 6. Let me give you an example.

In our learning community we were discussing the thrust of the creation narrative, Act 1 if you will. Of course, there was a rush to give the standard answers many of us reflexively parrot without really thinking. We had read the first eleven chapters of Genesis out loud and were focusing on the creation and garden narratives. When we started into our wiki-synthesis, Eric commented that this biblical account proved evolution didn't happen. Jill responded that she could appreciate the position but that she thought it may not prove anything about evolution and was actually a myth about how human consciousness came into being as something distinct from the instinctual living seen in the rest of the created order. Eric paused and allowed what Jill had said to sink in.

On a topic that can generate a lot of heat and with two positions so opposite, this could have been a moment of tense exchange that would jeopardize the creative space where improvisation could freely flow. To his credit Eric suspended judgment. He looked at Jill and said, "You know, Jill, I'm not sure I get it. Can you help me here? I don't understand a lot of what you just said, but I'm willing to try because I know if this is what you think, you must have good reasons. Will you explain it to me and all of us so I can feel and see what you feel and see?"

I was so proud of Eric. He's a pretty opinionated guy, but he had been in the learning community long enough to learn the skill of patient dialogue and see its fruit. He had been affected by it many times.

Jill went on to explain that she had been reading Eastern philosophy, which she found far fresher and more life-giving than the typical Christian reading, and she launched into a compelling, heartfelt understanding of the narratives. Eric's opening to Jill brought openness into the space and invited an openness in the other fifty people who were there. Jill ended her brief explanation by setting the tone for the next shift in our space. She said, "I guess I'm learning how different resources can creatively help me see and think about things I would have never considered before. For me to read thoughts about creation narratives from an Eastern Buddhist, a Jungian psychologist, and a Filipino feminist perspective has shown me how narrow my upbringing was and how little it has broadened as an adult. [Yes, Jill is well-read.] I realize a lot of deeply reflective and warmhearted people hold different views from me. I need to be patient to hear what they are saying."

What Jill said was something that people in many of the churches I have attended would have quickly shot down. But her words and heart created the next shift where the group, the acting troupe, began riffing and improvising on her themes. Jill created a kind of space that comes from a breadth of heart and a depth of understanding. She had been vulnerable to reveal how her narrowness had stunted her growth. In a compassionate way she opened her heart, which achieved something palpable in the group.

Over the next ninety minutes of discussion, one of the most amazing discussions I have ever been part of emerged, and yet it wasn't the only one that had taken place in this group. Group members had come to understand how to hold the creative improv space for each other and reproduce it at will. Compassion, understanding, and listening from a much wider space than self began to happen with regularity. We had biblically trained MDivs in the room, schoolteachers, full-time stay-at-home dads, a drill press operator, a lawyer, a physicist, several engineers, administrators, nurses, artists, a prison guard, and a host of people in other occupations. They all brought to the conversation something unique and valued.

Jill's comments set the space for creative interchange. People began asking the "what if" questions and exploring other ideas they had quietly harbored in their heads but never felt free to ask or talk about out loud. We had made several shifts in the listening space—moving from downloading what we hear to listening from the place of the other to listening to the wider field of the whole around us.

This wider field we might call "the kingdom space," the place where the Spirit of God was so evident to us. It was creative space where improv was happening and the coming to know new things was in full swing. Jesus came announcing an invisible realm, which was an ever-present, wider frame of reference in which everything we did was housed. Seeing and feeling this wider frame, this spacious place, is what we were beginning to experience in conversations.

The themes we discussed were many. We had extended riffs on shame. What was going on in Adam and Eve when all of a sudden their nakedness was an issue? What is shame, actually? What is shame in our culture, and how is it impacting us? Several people contextualized the shame conversation into their own lives. We left the biblical text for a while, riffing on personal stories, only to return to it later. We had conversations about human consciousness: How is it the same or different from animal consciousness? Plenty of people wanted to weigh in with stories about pets. What does all this mean as we are entering a time when some people think that computers, once they reach the speed and processing capacity of the human brain, may reach "consciousness"?[4]

As we listened to a wider field of the whole, *emergence* took place. All sorts of possibilities emerged that could have never been birthed in the creative improv space if "defending our position" were the main agenda. Without the principles of dialogue in place, we would have never come to know together, never have had so many insightful observations about the Genesis text, and never have learned a lot about ourselves and how exhilarating it is to share and hold that space for each other.[5]

As a pastor the greatest learning for me was the realization that while I have the degrees and commentaries and supposedly "right answers," none of them were as life giving, applicable, and resilient as the themes that emerged from our conversation that night. Everyone walked out of our art space (the place in which this learning community met) in awe of what had just happened. Unmistakably, the Spirit of God was energizing improvisation, insight, creativity, and imagination—and yet with an intention to be in continuity with the script-ure we were reading.

The act of participation itself was as life giving as the insights gleaned, which shouldn't be surprising. A great improv session with the jazz group or the drama troupe is life giving, no matter what the topic or takeaway. And yet it wasn't just energizing at the moment. We all noted a shelf life to our conversation far beyond the typical sage-on-stage experiences many of us were used to in our church settings. The chat board for the rest of the week was flying with applications, insights, and further riffing on the themes of the night. I had again experienced what it means to riff in the context of community and to come to know together.

I have had to learn that improvising in continuity with the script or score isn't as much about right and wrong ways of improvisation as about ways that release, echo, and creatively live into the fifth act. Some of these ways may have more heart or emotion or more authentically be in line with the plot or character development; others might be a bit shortsighted or less fully informed and therefore need to be brought more in line with the script. Faithful improvisation isn't about right and wrong. A drama script and a musical score just don't function that way.

This is where it begins to feel dangerous to many of us. People wonder what we will do when people start spouting heresy during public readings and conversations and start putting doctrinal nonsense out there.

It is a question I deeply relate to because it is the very one I used to ask when I was first challenged with this model. When we have been living with the owner's manual metaphor, then there is a right answer, a right application, a right way. For me, the question came from a place of my need to control and to make sure *the right answers* got out there. Reading the early church fathers and others from different time periods helped me in this struggle. I saw that throughout church history, people have had ideas that now appear loony.

My attempt at controlling what people think by correcting their misconceptions will not ensure the "sound doctrine" we often are so concerned about. We certainly need to do all we can in conversation to present what we think the drama script is saying. But presenting our thoughts and attempting to control the thoughts of others are rather different things. I know because I used to do a lot of the latter.

Several realizations have helped me loosen my control addiction. First, *I can't assume I have it all figured out*. At this stage in my learning, I am very convinced I don't. Things I used to be willing to take a bullet for are no longer even on the table as important. Part of it has to do with simple "stage of faith development" issues. Still, part of my job as a pastor and consultant is to be a step or three ahead of others on the journey, at least from the raw knowledge standpoint. It is important to me to help people see a picture of the drama script that is as whole, big, and clear as possible.

The issue is how we can best accomplish this. In the past we have looked to the expert to tell people what's what. This approach is an outgrowth of the lecture model of the Enlightenment rationalist world. We are learning, however, that most people do not learn best from lectures. The cognitive/sequential model of learning (a lecture or sermon, for example) engages only a minority of people. The brain dump, the dispensing of insightful nuggets, can be a legitimate starting point, but it can take us only so far and cannot help us with the "right doctrine" concern.

If controlling right doctrine is our main (or even secondary) goal, accomplished by constantly correcting and sealing off safe conversation spaces, aren't we violating the very principle of discovery, which is the foundation of all true learning? I am increasingly convinced that discovery doesn't happen optimally with monologue teaching/preaching.

Second, *I find that well-placed questions that allow people to draw out conclusions on their own give people insights that stick.* I don't give Ari, our tenth-grade daughter, the answer to her questions for her AP history homework. To give her the answer is to create dependency on me as the answer man. I do, however, ask her questions that help her learn the reading and synthesis skills necessary to see how Confucianism influenced Chinese politics and culture. The right answer is the secondary goal. Learning to read, process, and synthesize is the primary one. I have been the answer man, and I have loved playing it. Expert status was an ego trip. But it didn't help people dig in themselves. I created and fostered dependency on the very questions I could have reflected back to people or could have given them resources to investigate themselves.

Third, *I can't assume that the community as a whole doesn't have the insight to have self-stabilizing features built into it.* Wiki-synthesis has built into it the self-correcting features of patient community interaction. We have to learn to trust the work of the Holy Spirit in the community, and this is a perfect example. I admit this is something I have been learning slowly and at times painfully. But when you are on a journey with other people, it's the nature of the beast.

What is the alternative? Trusting one person who has read commentaries and the writings of other scholars to tell us what the text says? Is it better to have one person reading the Bible and books about the Bible and telling us his or her "right opinion," or to have all of us bring our reading skills and even reading the same books about the Bible and creating a shared understanding? Both share the same level of risk with regard to the doctrinal question. I'm just not convinced doctrinal purity was a top-shelf priority for Jesus. Just how much did the disciples actually know? My guess is that it's not nearly as much as we do.

THE ROLE OF OTHER ACTORS

Interacting with Script and Spirit

IN READING THE script-ure together, we come to see the big picture —the plot, story line, key characters, how later communities of faith enacted their improvisation in their contexts, and how different communities of faith did it differently. We then have to live into the fifth act.

This is a creative endeavor because some of the areas requiring improv have never been ventured into. We are looking at questions that may never have been faced by the church.

For instance, let's say a married couple at your church has infertility issues. And let's say they have been reading technical periodicals and have come across new research on using synthetically engineered sperm that is joined to the female ovum. They raise the question of whether their child will be fully human in God's eyes—since technology is playing half the role a parent usually would play? Or what if a forty-eight-year-old guy, whose dying parent is particularly brilliant, is invited to download the contents of his dad's brain onto a hard drive to later be uploaded to his. Or what if we move the experiments in cloning of a headless frog for froggy body part transplants into the realm of humans. How do we as a community of faith feel about cloning a headless me so I have a healthy organ bank of my "own" organs?

Now all of these things are still a tad sci-fi, but only a tad. Research and development on each of these scenarios is in full swing, and experts say their practice may be only a few short years away (some of it is already happening at a very basic level).

In our reflections about improvisation, we have to consider the issue of improvisation on questions the Bible hasn't even begun to address because of the social trajectory. Technology and medicine are on a steep innovation curve, and no doubt many of the developments are extremely helpful and valuable. But we would be blind to think there aren't unforeseen downsides. So how are we going to come up with answers to these ultra-sticky and complex issues?

I suggest that the community of actors, the Christ-followers we are doing life with, will be the conversations partners who improv on these very questions. I believe we can use the conversation arena to create a communitarian discernment dialogue in which we, over time, come to understand how we will converse about and sort out thorny questions all of us will have to face in one way or another.

The days are long gone when the pastor was one of the most educated persons in the community. Everyone in the community brings areas of interest, burning questions, and unique educational backgrounds that contribute to determining how we will live out and creatively improvise the fifth act.

Whether we are talking about shame in the context of Adam and Eve in Genesis (drama script-ure discussion), genetic engineering, the origins of the universe, or better education for our kids (improvising the fifth act in continuity with the script we have come to know together), all people need to be included and considered in the context of God's larger story for us and our world. The imagination and the creative interplay necessary to address these issues are substantial—and precisely why bringing the experience of the entire acting troupe into the conversation becomes so important.

Here's another example from our learning community. (This wasn't a typical church meeting, though some may have called it *church* quicker than they would our regular Sunday morning gathering, and it obviously wasn't a small group, not with sixty of us.) Over a three-week period, we watched "The Elegant Universe" DVD (a three-hour miniseries with Brian Greene) at the planetarium, and then had a conversation on origins of the universe with a professor of physics who is in our learning community. For another several weeks, we discussed how a theology of personhood is understood in the grand sweep of the biblical narrative with a lawyer in our community, who showed us how personhood is legally defined in our culture. Several educators in our community were burdened by the need for holistic education; so we had lengthy conversations about what holistic education includes. We reflected on what our reading of the drama script shows us about God, holism, and education, and on what the community could and should do to contribute to educating youth, especially at-risk youth.

We couldn't always go to a chapter and verse in the Bible to answer our questions. Nor could we turn to a pastor (me included) to answer these questions, because they were too varied and complex. We were asking questions smack-dab in the middle of our social, technological, and scientifically evolving world.

What did we do? We did what we did with the Genesis narrative: We opted for a model of community discussion, dialogue, and discernment that allowed a large group of people with various knowledge bases, interests, and concerns to enter into the questions and deep dialogue.

We need to realize what the Bible actually provides us: snapshots of various faith communities at various stages of social evolution working out their questions, issues, and concerns in the context of their knowledge of God and with the resources available to them. There are dramatic differences on every front between what the community of faith during Isaiah's prophecies knew and understood about God, what questions they were facing, and what resources were available to them and what was true for the people Paul was writing to in Philippi. Isaiah's community responded to their issues in ways that differed from the Philippian believers' responses. Maybe this truth can help us frame an insight as we continue to examine this idea of improvising the fifth act.

The Bible is not an owner's manual containing complete do-it-yourself instructions on how to make the machine of life in relationship to God hum well. No, it is a dramatic script capturing the journeys of a number of faith communities and God-followers throughout the last several thousand years who—based on their knowledge of God, the questions they were grappling with, and the social context in which they lived—improvised on living the abundant life of God. Isaiah's community and the Philippian community did different sorts of improv. After all, Philippi had a more complete script, a different knowledge about what the word God now meant, and a different understanding of how to live out in their context the implications of the incarnation.

We have multiple snapshots in the drama script. The cool part is they are not unrelated, discontinuous snapshots. All of these snapshots in the script-ure are on a continuous trajectory. Earlier bits of the script are picked up on and embellished by later communities that are featured in the script.

Improvisational dialogue will occur around the read-through of the drama script and the questions continually emerging in our context that the script couldn't have anticipated (genetics and technology, for example). The primary and third place of the improv conversation will happen in the context of living out the basics of character development inherent in being an improv actor for the fifth act.

DEEPLY ENGAGING THE SCRIPT

Ultimately, the place of real life is where we will need to know how to live out the script. Going to the grocery store, school, and workplace; navigating relationships and financial challenges; addressing the issues of homelessness in our community or illiteracy of kids in our schools—these are the things dominating our fifth-act contexts. What does all of this mean to those everyday situations?

In the truest sense of the word, we are talking about *genuine biblical education*—not just compiling, gathering, and managing data, but actually decompressing the information, breaking its code, and moving it to the place where it changes the way we live and interact in our world. Education isn't about teaching people *what* to think, which is how we have spent a lot of church time, but to help them learn *how* to think and respond appropriately in real time in continuity with the script-ure. I think we all ultimately hope our interaction with God's script provides this sort of transformative endpoint.

Information may be the starting point, but information injected into our heads will not necessarily bring about any change in our lives. This has been one of the problems with our current models of life change and biblical information transmission. We can give people a lot of information in a church service, and they often walk out excited about having learned a lot. That there is actual life change going on, however, may be more illusion than fact.

When I would ask people in the congregation I served for nearly eighteen years about how well last week's sermon "worked" in their lives, most people couldn't remember the title or the takeaways, let alone give concrete examples of application. My informal questioning during the past five years indicates more of the same. I may be indicting myself here, along with colleagues I know well and love deeply, but I am not convinced that ineffective pulpit skills are the culprit. I think we may have confused information with transformation. Reading the script will not help you improvise; it will only provide you the base from which you can improvise.

Plato said that when we focus too much on information, we create "imitators" or "tracers" instead of artists.[1] Alfred North Whitehead said that "a merely well-informed man is the most useless bore on God's earth."[2] We can study the script all we want, but it doesn't mean we will know how to improv the fifth act. The kinds of conversations on Scripture we have already talked about provide the groundwork for having the resources we need to move into the everyday realities we all face. How, then, does information become transformative?

GETTING PAST THE INFORMATION STARTING POINT

Educational theorist Tobin Hart believes information has to go through several levels of change before it can be transformational. He says that when we are talking about raw information, we are talking about discrete bits, bytes, and facts.[3] Information provides building blocks for other, more important systems we need if life change is to happen.

Information moves to knowledge when a learner starts constructing patterns of information. Knowledge implies the basic ability to use information. In school we may think of *information* as leaning about numbers—odd, even, and prime numbers. *Knowledge* is recognizing that whenever you add two even numbers, you always get an even sum. The deepest knowledge involves comprehension and mastery over a domain or skill. You might think math genius here.

Intelligence involves the ability to use information and knowledge and also the ability to create it. Intelligence shapes, changes, and constructs knowledge. The capacities for critical examination and evaluation open up closed systems of knowledge. Through the use of intelligence, knowledge and information can be taken out of context, recontextualized, and constructed for one's own uses. Think bridge builders who use calculus to calculate the volume of water flowing through a cylinder under the bridge. Intelligence is using the full faculties of the mind to transform information and knowledge into usable, complex, and contextualized applications.

When it comes to our Christian experience, many of us have a lot of information and knowledge and even some intelligence. As I reflect on most of the input into my life growing up as a Christian and during most of my life as a pastor, I see that I was primarily focused in the knowledge zone. I was taught to identify biblical patterns of God's interaction with people, to look at how these people responded (so we could respond in the same way—or not), and to construct a working model of how God's laws and rules of faith worked. And I often stopped right there. It is where most of my educational experience from grade school on stopped too. I know many educators who have told me the same thing, and I know plenty of pastors and Christians who feel trapped in the information game.

The goal in our biblical learning, in the preaching in our churches, in Bible studies, in our small groups, and in our discipleship relationships is often focused on mastering the domain of the

Bible: gather the critical biblical facts (information), put the information into a coherent system (knowledge), and then help people contextualize the mastered truth into their specific life contexts (intelligence). In reality, this approach has often fallen short of our goals of seeing real life change.

Tobin Hart says the next step is to move intelligence toward "understanding."[4] Understanding literally means "to stand among." The distance and boundary we create through our analysis need to be broken down. Studying and analyzing keep the Bible at arm's length. Our goal is to move toward intimacy and empathy with the biblical material and with those we are in dialogue with. The breakthrough that happens when we move from knowledge to understanding paves the way for a deep change in me.

At the understanding level, we are for the first time in the process moving from being the master of the script to allowing the script to master us. We can call this "the shift from head to heart," or we can call it "embodying the script." Whatever we call it, we realize this shift happens in all great "performances."

When I played jazz in high school, our instructor was always trying to get us to "feel" the improv. He would repeatedly tell us that we cannot think our way through the improv riff. We had to flow. When we hear a symphony, we recognize the difference between that which was technically adequate or even immaculate and the performance that merged the musicians with the music. This flow, this deep emergence from within, may be even more important when it comes to scripts and acting.

The well-known actor, director, and teacher Constantin Stanislavski, is renowned for his development of what is called the Stanislavski system—a way of learning how to act that embodies in the fullest sense possible the script being performed.[5] His goal was to have his actors as fully as possible "live into" their characters based on the roundtable conversations they had—conversations that occur among all the actors about their understanding of the script, its trajectory, the characters in the script, and so forth.

Stanislavski would have them do a read-through, and they would do what we have been calling a wiki-synthesis: everyone weighing in with their thoughts and observations about the shape of the script and their understanding of the writer's goals and intent. Roundtable discussions after a script read-through were the precursor to the actual performance. The conversation was important because the actors were coming to know together. They were amassing the necessary information and knowledge and trying to determine how they would contextualize the script in their performance—*intelligence* in Hart's model discussed above.

What they hadn't yet done was live out the script. To do that they would have to let the script enter them, and they would have to allow the other performers' performances to "get inside them." Stanislavski required a "total dedication—encompassing body, mind, and soul—to the role."[6] He believed the key to a performer's inhabiting a role in the script wasn't about makeup, hair, props, or costumes; it was about an "inner preparation."[7]

Hart calls this inner preparation "understanding." We move from head to heart, from mind to soul, from knowing to embodying, from two-dimensional to three-dimensional. Martin Buber, the great Jewish philosopher, says, "All real living is meeting."[8] When we are talking about understanding, we are talking about this activity of *meeting*. Understanding requires a fundamental shift in the way we know. It is more visceral and has deep emotive dimensions. The move to understanding is underway when we press into the script and the other actors, when we suspend our subject/object distance and separateness created through analysis. When we are willing to take this risk, the music flows through us, the script lives through us, the community improvises with us. In this new and risky space we find an appreciation and openness, and we begin listening from a new place and with a permeating love because of the environment created.

UNDERSTANDING AND EMOTION: THE FUEL OF IMPROV

"The essential difference between emotion and reason is that emotion leads to action while reason leads to conclusions."[9] This quote is attributed to Donald Calne, a neurophysiologist, who helps us realize that our actions are tied to deep emotions. The fact that his insight is quoted in a marketing textbook makes sense. Marketers realize that we don't make most purchases based on a cognitive evaluation of a product's ingredients; our purchase is usually based on a feeling. In other words, we act based on something a bit more squishy than rational evidence.

For a long time we have elevated reason to the pinnacle. We often assume that reason is primary and emotion a subset. We find out, however, that we are first and foremost emotional creatures who develop the subset of reason as we progress through life.[10] I wonder if this insight points to one of the reasons we have sometimes come up short in experiencing transformational change in our spiritual lives. I have often been so cognitive that feelings may have never entered into the equation. I have excelled up to the intelligence rung but never quite made it to the "understanding" stage, which requires emotional engagement.

Calne challenges us to get our improvising to a place fueled by emotion. Only a shift from head to heart will move us from knowing to doing, or, to quote the biblical writer James, from hearing to doing (see James 1:22). We need to *feel* our way into our life situations. If we merely acquire the information, we will draw conclusions but will not understand or proceed to action. We may be intelligent and have amassed a bunch of historical background knowledge and facts, but we are not experiencing the script-ure and will therefore be unable to improvise. We may parrot or recite, but we won't improvise. Of course, this becomes important not just to me living out the script but to those around me as well.

Understanding is an all-out call to return to no-boundary existence and to enter into life in an arena where we are one with the story we are living out and one with those we are doing our fifth-act living with. Here is real community, real com-unity. It is hard for me not to think this is what Jesus meant and was praying for in John 17. I really don't think he was referring to the disciples' sharing a doctrinal oneness or a unity in their belief system. To do so would be to read John 17 through our typical lens of analysis and modern intellectual frameworks.

Jesus is asking the Father to give the disciples a sense of *deep interconnection*, the same thing Paul is pointing to when he uses the body of Christ metaphor. The body of Christ is a no-boundary metaphor. We live as one community in which I really do feel your pain, I do riff and play off of your strengths, I do support and encourage — because we share the same blood vessels and "heart."

WORKING EXAMPLES
Riffing the Script

AT ONE TIME or another, we have all felt out of place. The first day of school is a good example. Whether it was the first day of kindergarten, high school, or college, the feelings were essentially the same. I think about my first day in high school and remember how overwhelmed I was. The world I was going into was so much bigger than my previous world. Would I get lost? How would I move from one class to the next? Do I have enough time to do all this without getting lost? And what if I look stupid? I'm one of the cool kids; I can't look stupid. I had a feeling of excitement mixed with fear—*anxiety* isn't a bad description. I just wanted to make sure I fit in.

Sound familiar?

I have had the same experience numerous times as I've gone into remote international airports where there are no signs in English and few, if any, English speakers. I remember getting off an airplane in Irkutsk—Russian Siberia. Did I ever feel out of place!

I also felt fearful, freezing cold, unsure of myself, alone, and even disoriented. How do you find out where you need to go when no one speaks your language, when you see no signs in your language, and you have no one coming to pick you up?

FRETFUL IN PHILIPPI

Some communities of faith who are trying to improv their fifth act understand these feelings of being out of place. The Philippian community is a great example of a group feeling out of place. They had substantial anxiety and feelings of disorientation. They were being asked to step into a new reality and to show those around them what it meant to live the values of an invisible world—and to do all this in the spirit of the example of their master, who had made a strategic and intentional choice to feel out of place and dislocated.

This group's mentor, Paul, fully understood what it felt like to be out of place. It was the story of his life on a number of different fronts. Using his experience, he wrote them a letter of encouragement to help them come to grips with their anxiety, their sense of feeling out of place, and to remind them that, no matter how things looked, the kingdom progress marches on in subversive and quiet ways. Paul used Jesus as an example of one who did the ultimate out-of-place thing for the community.

Let's take the book of Philippians as a test case and consider how we would read it under the "learning to improv" model instead of the "extract and apply" model.[1]

Begin by reading through the book of Philippians in its entirety. (It will take you about fifteen to twenty minutes.) Any translation you have is fine. If you are an experienced Bible reader, you might be at a slight disadvantage because you are reading with "pre-understanding," with the lenses we have heard about throughout this book. You will need to be especially careful about what you read into the narrative on this pass and what you allow to come out of the script-ure as you "read it again for the first time."

Resist the temptation to pause over favorite verses or to get distracted by how the text might apply to you today. Read the book as a letter to a faith community you are eavesdropping on. You are reading a slice of *their* story. Remember that this was a book written by Paul to a particular people of God in a Roman colony named Philippi. They had a particular understanding of God, specific issues they were facing, and explicit questions they were asking. You are reading their story to understand exactly these things about *their* story.

As you read, think about the idea of "subject matter." What is the subject matter of Philippians? Note the things this community is dealing with, some of their values, the challenges they are up against, the approach they are taking or are being instructed to take. Look for broad brushstrokes. Refer back to the questions in chapter 13 (pp. 158–59), if that would be helpful. (The goal isn't to read and then answer each question as if this were a fill-in-the-blank quiz. The point is to allow these questions to provide you with a new set of lenses as you read.)

So hit the pause button and go read the whole letter of Paul to the Philippians.

Welcome back! Any big-picture ideas emerge?

I will begin by making some brief comments to kick off the conversation about how the book of Philippians provides us with clues about how we can improvise the next chapter of God's unfolding kingdom through us today. Perhaps this will give you a new, more helpful way of thinking about how Scripture should be approached.

Remember, as a next step it would be ideal if you could read this out loud with a group of people and do a wiki-synthesis of everyone's observations. After I share a few of my own observations, I will move on to record some of the observations I heard in a group that read Philippians together.

A Few Personal Observations

Philippians was a letter written to a church that Paul apparently founded (see Acts 16:9–40). Paul doesn't come right out and tell us exactly why he wrote the letter, but several facts can be deduced by reading the contents of the letter carefully. Paul writes the letter from prison and wants the Philippians to know that even though he is relatively sure of the outcome of his imprisonment, they need to know it's all good. He sees that even his imprisonment is working out just as God had planned and that his message is advancing in the prison to those around him, the very message he was imprisoned for spreading in the first place.

Like all good stories, and Paul's life is surely that, we are thrust neck-deep into details of intrigue and wonder as we seek to understand not only what he wrote but the details he omitted. He wants the Philippians to realize that unity is important in the midst of false teaching challenges (Philippians 3:2) and relational friction (4:2). Paul encourages them with a call to rejoice, no matter what their circumstances, for rejoicing is his posture even in prison. Paul is writing also to thank them for financial support (4:14–18) and care for him.

As we consider why Paul wrote Philippians, it is interesting to note just how historically bound the book feels. The book is talking about things that seem to have little, if any, bearing on us. Imprisoned for a religious message? This would have happened to Paul not because he did something illegal but as a peace-keeping measure—a very different sort of scenario from our understanding of "prison." In this type of situation you had to have someone take care of your basic needs in prison. Your guards didn't feed you and supply your needs; that was up to your family and friends. We also get a little insight into a community where false teachers may have been misleading a small group of people.

These things are removed from us by nearly two thousand years. An entirely different language, culture, political context, and understanding of God make the situation foreign to us—which is precisely why getting the broad brushstrokes is so important.

Many themes emerge as you read the book the first time through. Multiple readings, conversations, and adjustments of our understanding are important because one pass probably isn't enough to really get the internal logic of the letter.

Reading in Community

Let's take a stab at a couple things that seem obvious to me and to some of the people I have read the letter aloud with.

One thing we can notice from the 50,000-foot view is the repeated theme of *feeling out of place*; we might call it *dislocation* or *disorientation*. Paul mentions individuals who have been removed from their normal comfortable surroundings and put into odd, difficult, challenging, or stretching environments. Paul shows people who "aren't at home" in the situations and circumstances they find themselves in and how these people dealt with and handled these situations of being out of their element. Paul helps the Philippians see the appropriate way to respond to displacement.

I can't quote a specific verse about dislocation per se. The work of synthesis is precisely the effort of trying to tie together the things we see, not necessarily parrot the words we read. We are trying to identify themes that keep popping up in the letter and therefore must be the things Paul meant to highlight. You can feel the difference in reading Philippians this way as compared to scouring the passage for pithy formulas or truths to apply.

The wiki-synthesis conversation (or the roundtable conversation Stanislavski made his actors endure after completing a script read-through) is exactly what we are doing here. Reading Scripture in a group is so much more fun, enlightening, and helpful than reading alone.

Imagine the Philippians getting this letter from Paul. Paul didn't send a separate email or fax (or mail) a hard copy to each member of the church. Someone presumably received the letter and then read the whole thing to the church at their next gathering. I don't think it would be a stretch to think that the letter might have been read several times or that particular sections were read repeatedly. I can picture someone in the small house church saying, "Hey, can you read that section again right after the song Paul quotes?" (Philippians 2:6–11 is considered an early church hymn.) Chapter and verse references were not put into these texts for nearly a thousand years.

In this exercise we are trying to grab hold of overarching pieces of the story, of which there may be several. We are trying to see what big ideas keep emerging (theological reflection) and then figure out if there is a way for us to piece them all together (open source or wiki-community) into some cohesive pattern or whole (synthesis). I know this all sounds a bit technical and fancy, but this reading approach constantly pushes us to view things from a higher altitude. The old approach tended to drill down past the forest *and* the trees to the blades of grass on the forest floor.

We are ultimately looking to answer this question: How can the story of the Philippians and their interaction with their world (necessary step #1) provide me some clues for how I am to improvise being Jesus to those around me?

Let's return to the idea of displacement and dislocation.

In the opening sections of the book, *Paul notes that he is displaced.* He is in prison for proclaiming the message of the gospel.

Paul has been put into a situation where he is stripped of all free-doms. His goal of making the gospel known appears to be thwarted, and he clearly now must rely on and look to others. As we are drawn into Paul's story, we can see how anger and outrage might be the obvious response. You have probably seen TV shows and news-casts of people who were mistakenly or unjustly imprisoned, or maybe you experienced it yourself—and you remember the emotions you felt. Thinking about the years of life Paul lost and sensing the unbelievable pain he had to endure draw us into the story line.

We realize the natural human response Paul could give in this context isn't the one he gives. Humility, quiet confidence, and trust constitute his response. The interesting and certainly unintended consequence of Paul's imprisonment was that the very gospel that he was being imprisoned for preaching was quietly and yet perceptibly advancing. This might be considered illustration number one of the idea Paul puts forth in his overarching and sweeping opening state-ments to the Philippians: *God has begun a work in the community of the Philippians and will continue that work and even bring it to climax.* Paul starts his letter this way because it is the informing life force he has come to know in his own life about the God he serves. He wants the Philippians to see his underlying assumption about God's activity. We might note this is one of the worldview pieces for Paul.

The very gospel Paul's enemies were trying to silence was marching on. This isn't surprising to Paul, because *what God starts he finishes.* God is like a bulldog on this stuff who won't let a bit of opposition thwart things. For God and for Paul, quiet reversal hap-pens even in the midst of the humble feeling of being out of place. Because of Paul's confidence in how God works in these situations, his disposition is joy—a deep and settled sense of lightness and peace. We aren't far into the Philippian story, and already we see how reading at a higher altitude can be helpful.

A second dislocation happens quickly on the heels of the opening sections. Paul's primary example in the story line of the Philippians is to bring to them the lyrics of a song they sing, a song about the *dislocation and displacement of Jesus* — his death, and then his resurrection and exaltation. Philippians 2:6 – 11 is called a hymn in New Testament scholarship and is the most well-known one in the Bible. We have a story we are reading in letter form; embedded in that letter Paul quotes lyrics to a song.

This may or may not be important to note, but it does tell us that this hymn probably is substantial. It has a life of its own apart from Paul using it as an illustration in his letter. The hymn shows Jesus in a place of total peace, joy, and, we might even say, comfort. He chose to be displaced, willingly and knowingly, so he could accomplish something more important than maintaining and holding on to undisrupted ease. He "did not consider equality with God something to be used to his own advantage," the text says (Philippians 2:6).

As we were doing our read-through and wiki-synthesis, Lori noted how this song looks like a reversal of the story of Adam in creation. Adam was in the form of God, but thought being even more like God was something to be pursued. Instead of humbling himself, he exalted himself, and instead of experiencing resurrection life, he brought about death. She also made the connection that Adam faced forced displacement from the garden, setting up the human condition as one of feeling "not at home" — alienated and out of place.

Lori was making a connection between this story, the book of Philippians, and the larger overarching themes we find in the whole of the script-ure. This particular connection was important because it tied the Philippians hymn into the primal story of creation and Adam. Lori's observation is something that scholars have discussed for a long time as "Adam Christology" and is seen in passages in which Paul compares Adam and Christ.[2]

Her observations fueled excellent group conversation. Many people noted that they had never seen the connection before. As a result of Lori's sharing, the group got to riff on the text of Genesis and the Adam/Jesus comparison.

Jesus' dislocation was voluntary, downward, humbling. He displayed downward mobility in a world where upward mobility is the direction we want to go. The hymn in Philippians speaks of an ironic reversal. The Jesus who died "taking the very nature of a servant" (Philippians 2:7) is the one everyone must eventually bow to (2:10). Humbling, downward dislocation again leads to quiet reversal. And the reversal is not only personal for Jesus; it is global and universal as well. Lori's comment that Jesus made good on what Adam messed up is exactly right.

Paul was in prison and Jesus came to earth—both out-of-place situations, both dislocations with ironic reversals. Paul's imprisonment spread the gospel he was being imprisoned for spreading, and Jesus' humbling is what led every knee to ultimately bow to him.

Paul's dislocation out of his heritage to a world no longer defined by ethnicity, law keeping (a dominant definer of purity among the Jews), *and external signs of belonging* (such as circumcision) is a third example in the letter of not being at home any longer. Paul's point here is that if anyone had the right to feel confident in his life, his direction, and his "rightness" on the basis of any of these external symbols, it certainly would be Paul. He was the best in class. He believed in his position so much he was willing to watch and perhaps preside over the first recorded martyrdom in the New Testament (Acts 8:1).

But all of Paul's certainty changed. He didn't feel at home anymore in that old world. He was being displaced and relocated into a "new world"; he was being redefined by new standards, new values, and new goals. Paul was experiencing his own downward dislocation. He went from being the top dog in law keeping — the word he used was "faultless" (Philippians 3:6) — to a place where law keeping meant absolutely zero. Paul had been humbly displaced into a new kind of life. The old life was essential to help Israel become pure and ready for the coming of the Messiah; Paul's new life was resituated in an ironic reversal as he now proclaimed Jesus as King, the very Jesus he once killed people for following (Acts 7:57 – 8:3; 9:1 – 2).

The fourth sweeping displacement theme has to do with the Philippians, who were *Roman citizens but who didn't live in Rome.* Paul plays on this dislocation theme in Philippians 3. Philippi is a Roman colony — which essentially meant you could live as a full Roman citizen in this remote, "displaced" location. The full rights of Roman citizenship were yours as a citizen of Philippi, even though you were not geographically residing within the city limits of Rome. Maybe you can start to see where this is going. It seems unmistakable that Paul wants us to realize that *following Christ means we will never feel totally at home.* We will always feel out of place at multiple levels, and not feeling quite at home will always bring with it a resituating of our lives and will influence how we view ourselves and our purpose for being here, how we interact with and address the world we find ourselves in.

A final dislocation theme dovetails with the previous one and completes the picture Paul is sketching. Just as the Philippian Christians were displaced geographically and yet were Roman citizens, *they were also displaced in physical ways from their true home with God.* Their citizenship wasn't ultimately with Rome but with God in heaven (Philippians 3:20). The Philippians experienced a double dislocation, as Roman citizens in Philippi and as Christians not yet fully at their eternal destination but living on this earth as double agents. And this living on earth while having citizenship in heaven means that the gospel advances in quiet and mysterious ways through the Philippians, an alternative community on planet Earth. The advance of the gospel in this "not being at home yet" displacement is ironic too.

These three dovetail into a highly charged political connection. If Jesus is King, then this means, quite simply, that Caesar is not. Here is the tension though: Caesar *is* the king in Rome; and because Philippi is a Roman colony, he *is* king in Philippi as well. While Paul points out the humility of Christ's downwardly mobile move and the need for the Philippians to emulate his attitude, it seems he might be saying something even more political in quoting the hymn in chapter 2. Paul is no dummy. He couldn't come right out and make an obvious statement. Instead he makes covert and subversive statements about where the real allegiance of the Philippian Christians must lie.

When the hymn says that "every knee should bow ... and every tongue acknowledge that Jesus Christ is Lord [King]," Paul knows full well that one of Caesar's titles is Lord, and that Roman citizens had to honor him as Lord. For Paul to quote this hymn, which crescendos with "Jesus Christ is Lord," is boldness of the highest sort. For him to write this to the Philippians, who as a Roman outpost had to pay homage to Caesar, is nothing short of an "in your face, Caesar" statement from Paul—and a strong statement about the Philippians' out of placeness. Paul is essentially giving the Philippians guidance on how they were to improv living out the gospel and being the risen Jesus when they were living as physical citizens in a Roman outpost—when their real citizenship wasn't in Rome, or even in Philippi.

As you read Philippians, you may or may not have caught the dislocations and feelings of not being at home discussed here. It may or may not have struck you that the displacements had facets of downward mobility, humility, ironic reversal, and subversive twists. But given the repetition of the theme in the Philippian story, these facets seem to be clear emphases of Paul.

Are these the *only* themes? Is this the best way to summarize the story of Philippians? The beauty of story is how it is tolerant of many layers of observations. Wiki-synthesis gives us the insights of the many in the community. Allowing the whole group to enter into conversation creates the push-and-pull space for us to come to know together. My experience in these roundtable, read-through dialogues is the rich addition to my understanding of all the deep, full, and informed observations of others I would have missed if I had read alone.

ASKING THE BIGGER QUESTIONS

As we understand the contours of the Philippian story, we can begin to pose the questions from chapter 13. What do these themes tell us about God and our understanding of his story and of the bigger story of stories?

When we asked this question in our group, Clark said he noticed something fascinating as he was listening to the out-loud reading of Philippians 2. In verses 14–15 Paul encouraged the community with these words: "Do everything without grumbling or arguing, so that you may become blameless and pure, children of God without fault in a warped and crooked generation. Then you will shine among them like stars in the sky."

Clark said, "I've been reading large sequential blocks through the Pentateuch (the first five books of the Old Testament, Genesis through Deuteronomy). The idea of not grumbling and arguing is rooted in the Old Testament story of Israel's grumbling and arguing when she was displaced and dislocated.[3] And let me read something I read just this week as I was finishing Deuteronomy." Clark proceeded to read Deuteronomy 32, where Israel is called warped, crooked, and perverse because they have not been the people of God they were supposed to be.

Clark had made connections to this story of the Philippian people of God and the story of Israel as the Old Testament people of God. He had seen themes emerge around the idea of displacement and dislocation that he hadn't seen before. The Israelites as a displaced people were grumblers and were called warped, crooked, and perverse. Paul's echoing of these words here highlight how the Philippian story has continuity with the Old Testament people of God (Israel) but also has unique dimensions only the Philippians would encounter.

Because Clark had been reading big blocks of Old Testament material, he was starting to see the big sweeping story of Israel and how common the theme of being out in unknown territory was for the people of God. He was also seeing how easy it was to grumble about the unknown—a grumbling that accompanies the dislocation from the comfort and ease we so often default to. Clark made this connection for the group and helped us see the displacement as a people connection as well.

TIME TO IMPROV

What was left was to ask how the response of the people in God's story who were experiencing these disorienting dislocations could inform our learning about how to improv the next act of that story line in our world here and now.

We are not at home. We feel out of place and dislocated as Christ-followers. We are on foreign terrain, and there we have been invited to broker the kingdom of God. Maybe we aren't in prison; maybe we don't live in a satellite location that gives us city privileges. Maybe none of the specifics of the text apply; they don't need to. The script-ure wasn't meant to give us specific applications at that "drill down into the details of the text" level. But the text does give us great application at the 50,000-foot view. We *are* dislocated as Christ-followers. And with dislocation comes a resituating.

I wonder if the book of Philippians is intended to help us come to grips with dislocation and the way we are to live as a resituated alternative community. What if the book has been given to get us talking about what our dislocation feels like, complete with all the surrounding emotions? And what if the book is a glimpse into how we might deal with feeling alienated, alternative, and on the margins, like foreigners living with the values of another "location" — a location from which we have been displaced? How do we live the countercultural values of humility and downward mobility in the face of the American Dream story in which we are immersed? What is downward mobility in our world right now?

The questions that arise in our community conversation are what will help us understand how we are to do our improvisation.

Dan, a businessman in our group, said he had been thinking about Paul's imprisonment. He asked the group one night, "Have you ever done what you thought was right, lived out values with integrity and honesty, only to be marginalized or sidelined because of it? I think this happens often in the marketplace. We try to live values that model Jesus and kingdom priorities, but there is no reward for that; in fact, it often feels like it backfires." He was noting this was precisely what Paul had experienced.

Here is one of the repeated themes: we cannot expect rewards from the world around us when we are living a value system out of sync with that world. The good news is that while dislocation stinks at one level, *God's kingdom is advancing* in quiet, subterranean ways. Your humility and joy in the midst of feeling unrewarded is part of the catalyst for the imperceptible but certain march of God's love, care, and kingdom. For Dan, this was helpful grist as a new believer.

The conversation we had in our group about Philippians circled around all these questions and more. We had quite a discussion about what it meant to be an alternative people when we all felt the gravitational pull of "getting ahead." Several people noted how we have often been told that if we live God's way, by his values, then we will get ahead, be monetarily blessed, climb the ladder of success. And there may be cases in which this is true; there were some even in our group for which this was true. The beauty of community, though, is there are always counterexamples. We had a number of people for whom the life of Paul or Job were closer analogies than the living out of the American Dream.

The message of Philippians for all of us in the group was that feeling out of sync with the prevailing climate of the day was not only OK but important if we were to be the bright and shining lights we were invited to be. It was the model Jesus gave us. It is what Paul experienced. And it was the up-close and personal experience of a whole faith community at Philippi. Can we find strength and comfort in knowing that God's work courses on when we live in continuity with otherworld values that displace us in this one? Are we OK about knowing that our being faithful, humble, and willing may move us off the success ladder of the American Dream—and that this is exactly how God's work can flow on in mysterious ways?

Philippians was a great conversation piece for us. The twenty-first-century church needs to think through what it means to improvise the next act of God's drama, to write the next chapter of his story in our community and in continuity with what we have read. Philippians helped all of us realize that feeling out of place is the normal experience of Jesus' alternative community; this feeling is part of what it means for us to be the people of God. Our community was learning in our read-through times and wiki-synthesis dialogues *how* the Bible was "useful for teaching, rebuking, correcting and training in righteousness," to quote 2 Timothy 3:16. How it was useful was quite different in this discussion from the way most of us had been taught before. We were beginning to see familiar passages in a new light. "Continue to work out your salvation with fear and trembling" (Philippians 2:12) had nothing to do with the Philippians trying to figure out how to get to heaven but with being rescued from a difficult situation.[4]

Terry noticed that the context of the whole book required that we see the super-Christian passage of "I can do all this through [Christ] who gives me strength" in the light of the perseverance, the staying power, Paul had in the face of suffering and being displaced because of being a Jesus-follower. Terry laughed as she admitted that this wasn't the way she had applied the passage for most of her life. She used it as a magical mantra whenever she wanted to accomplish something she thought was hard. She totally understood now for the first time why the verse never seemed to really "work."

So what is the big-picture takeaway? If we are called to improvise the next part of the story—and remember that in this entire book I have been trying to show that the goal is not to recite, memorize, or reenact the biblical story; our goal is to *extend the biblical story into our time*—then Philippians encourages us to accept this out-of-place feeling as part of our gig.

The beautiful thing about improvising is realizing the communitarian nature of the art form. I improvise in community with others who are part of the acting troupe or musical ensemble. We play off each other, we learn from each other, we embellish on each other's enactments, we create a new part of the story—a new part deeply in continuity with the biblical story but moving beyond the biblical story because the issues of our day, the questions of our time, the problems we face, have no chapter and verse to be given as answers.

I think the biggest thing this improvising model offers is a life lived in an alternative story line. Conversion is a daily experience as I continue the slow but sure relinquishment of my personal story line, which for me is highly influenced by the American Dream. We see Paul doing this in Philippians 3, where his personal story is swapped for a bigger, fuller, more purposeful, and "aligned with God" story. This is conversion of a deeper, more nuanced sort than the abbreviated "make Jesus the Lord of your life." I am all for making Jesus Lord; I just think there is a lot more involved.

On the one hand, the story of Philippians challenges the hyperindividualism of my American Dream story line (hence "community"); on the other hand, it causes me to rethink the values that attend to my current story line in light of being an *alternative* community. As an alternative community, we will bring to bear, quite literally, an out-of-this-world set of values that we can bring to the conversations and issues we face.

Improvisation is a learned art form. And an art form it is. It requires community conversation and participation. It requires immersion in the biblical story so that our improvisation is in continuity with the story told so far. And then it requires a creative and imaginative grappling with the questions of our time, so that the biblical story extends and expands as we model how to live as the people of God in this new time. We seek continuity with the past and creative engagement with today, immersion with the text as written and imagination for how to live the next chapters of that text today.

I often think back to the high school days of Study. What a ride and a rush! Those guys and gals with whom I cut my biblical teeth have indelibly marked my life. I think about the tattoo conversation with Keith and the insights of Tara reminding us that if Keith can't get a tattoo, then we shouldn't be wearing our band uniforms. Those were the first efforts at improvisation and wiki-synthesis for me. Each step on the journey has been a critical step in faith development and understanding how the Bible is a shaping, molding force in our lives. Let me invite you into the community and the art of improv. You will never read or live the same way again.

NOTES

Chapter 2: The Tattoo Incident

1. A concordance lists every instance of a particular word in the Bible. If you want to find each usage of the word *righteous* in the Bible, this is the resource you need, whether online or in a big reference book.

Chapter 3: Presbyterian, Catholic, and Charismatic

1. See Luke 6:38 ("Give, and it will be given to you") and 2 Corinthians 9:6 or Galatians 6:7–8 on reaping and sowing.
2. See Deuteronomy 28–32; Malachi 3:10. Read "financial blessing."
3. Think Luke 18:29.
4. The Bible uses many metaphors and images that aren't necessarily intended to be taken literally. In Psalm 139:8, which reads, "If I go *up* to the heavens . . . ," spatial language is being used. Heaven may not literally be "up" from where we are currently located. Understanding how these figures of speech are used and what they are communicating falls within the domain of hermeneutics — the academic area of rules and theories of interpretation. I will examine the essentials of hermeneutics in greater detail in chapter 6.

5. Webster's dictionary defines *anthropomorphism* as "an interpretation of what is not human or personal in terms of human or personal characteristics."

Chapter 5: Selective Application

1. I went to Trinity Evangelical Divinity School for my master's studies. Scot McKnight was my primary mentor. His book *The Blue Parakeet* (Zondervan, 2008) chronicles his journey on the question and some of the heat generated by those debates.
2. In all fairness, I know there are people who believe we should sell all we have and live commune style. My friend Shane Claiborne is one well-known example of someone who embraces a countercultural living out of this injunction.

Chapter 7: Faith and Human Development

1. James Fowler, *Becoming Adult, Becoming Christian* (San Francisco: Jossey-Bass, 2000).
2. Ibid., 40.
3. The importance of these ideas will emerge in the next chapter when we look at how our view of God and the Bible are in a mutually defining dance.
4. Fowler, *Becoming Adult*, 44.
5. See David Rooke and William R. Torbert, "The Seven Transformations of a Leader," *Harvard Business Review* 83 (April 2005): 66–77.
6. See Robert Kegan, *In Over Our Heads: The Mental Demands of Modern Life* (Cambridge, Mass.: Harvard Univ. Press, 1998), 128–34.
7. Fowler, *Becoming Adult*, 49.
8. Ibid., 51.
9. For an accessible explanation of the move in science from certainty to uncertainty, see David Lindley, *Uncertainty: Einstein, Heisenberg, Bohr, and the Struggle for the Soul of Science* (New York: Anchor, 2008).
10. Fowler, *Becoming Adult*, 52.
11. See Arthur Holmes, *All Truth Is God's Truth* (Downers Grove, Ill.: InterVarsity, 1983).

Chapter 8: View of God/View of Scripture

1. N. T. Wright, *The New Testament and the People of God* (Minneapolis: Fortress, 1992), 121–44.
2. Ibid., 123–24.
3. Kelsey (*Proving Doctrine* [Harrisburg, Pa.: Trinity Press, 1999]) argues that all theologians make a basic move prior to trying to prove their doctrinal position or theological agenda. He says they all decide *how* the Bible will be used as authoritative in supporting their particular arguments. He calls this their "construal" of Scripture.
4. Kelsey, *Proving Doctrine*, 167.
5. Mircea Eliade, *Shamanism: Archaic Techniques of Ecstasy* (New York: Pantheon, 1964), 3–4. For a fascinating detailing of shamanism as a precursor to what we see in many religious contexts, see Robert Wright, *The Evolution of God* (New York: Little, Brown and Company, 2009), 29–45.
6. Walter Brueggemann, *The Word That Redescribes the World* (Minneapolis: Augsburg, 2006), 3.
7. Ibid., 4.
8. Ibid., 5.

Chapter 9: Shifting Our View of the Bible

1. Anthony Thistelton, *New Horizons in Hermeneutics* (Grand Rapids: Zondervan, 1997), 352.
2. I have already noted how the instructions to young men in Titus 2:6–8, one of my early memorized verses, are followed with instructions on how slaves should respond to their masters.
3. See Deuteronomy 7 or Numbers 31:15–18, that disquieting passage in which everyone is to be killed but the virgins, who are to be kept for the troops.
4. This doesn't even begin to touch the issue of why homosexuality is often singled out in the Romans 1 passage. Greed, envy, deceit, gossip, and arrogance are mentioned as outcomes of depravity, right alongside homosexuality—yet these sins don't seem to generate the same heat or vigor in the church as the homosexual issue does.

Chapter 10: New Metaphors for the Shift

1. David Tracy, in a profoundly insightful book (*The Analogical Imagination* [New York: Herder and Herder, 1998]), was the first person I've read to suggest the fascinating metaphor of a *classic* for how the Bible and our Christian tradition exercise authority in our lives. Tracy goes to great pains to help his readers realize that *how* they read the text and what they are looking for in the text have specific predictable outcomes. When we read the Bible as doctrine, we see lots of doctrinal material. When we read the Bible as a list of prescriptive rules, we see many of them to apply. In this way, Tracy's observations are similar to those of David Kelsey.
2. Tracy, *Analogical Imagination*, 99.
3. Ibid., 102 – 7.
4. Ibid., 101.

Chapter 11: The Drama Script

1. N. T. Wright, "How Can the Bible Be Authoritative?" *Vox Evangelica* 21 (1991):7 – 32, *http://www.ntwrightpage.com/Wright_Bible_Authoritative.htm* (accessed April 14, 2009). Though Wright is not the only or even first to suggest this way of seeing our interaction with the biblical text, his is certainly the most elegant explanation. For those who want to delve into academic treatments of this idea of drama, theo-drama, and our being a part of God's theater, see Hans Urs von Balthasar's five-volume work *Theo-Drama: Theological Dramatic Theory* (Fort Collins, Colo.: Ignatius, 1988 – 98). For a different take, see Kevin Vanhoozer, *The Drama of Doctrine* (Louisville: Westminster, 2005).
2. Wright, "How Can the Bible Be Authoritative?" 19.
3. Ibid., 20.
4. Vanhoozer, *Drama of Doctrine*, 17. Vanhoozer's book is, quite honestly, breathtaking, but it is such a lengthy and cumbersome volume that it will never reach most pastors, let alone the average person in the pew. See his own admission in the preface: "Some of the energy that I hope to communicate in this book may be overshadowed by its mass. I had originally intended to write a short, constructive

manifesto." The mass of the volume? Nearly 500 pages (with 86 footnotes in the introduction alone)! And so it is that many pastors and people in our faith communities never interact with this kind of material. A book such as this feels removed from the everyday bump and grind of ministry and life because it looks, reads, and feels so academic. With books of this mass and density, we are not likely to make inroads into overturning tired paradigms at the practical level. We will continue to have these conversations at academic conventions but not in many churches. Vanhoozer is a winsome writer with profound and important things to say. Sadly, I haven't met one pastor of the hundreds I work with each year who has even heard of the book.

Chapter 12: Immersing in the First Four Acts

1. Daniel Boorstin, *The Discoverers* (New York: Random House, 1983), 86.
2. See Arien Mack and Irvin Rock, *Inattentional Blindness* (Cambridge, Mass.: MIT Press, 2000).
3. Margaret Wheatley, *Turning to One Another* (San Francisco: Berrett-Koehler, 2002), 3.

Chapter 13: The Role of the "Acting Community"

1. See Shane Hipps, *The Hidden Power of Electronic Culture* (Grand Rapids: Zondervan, 2006). This book has been rewritten with more application for life (*Flickering Pixels: How Technology Shapes Your Faith* [Grand Rapids: Zondervan, 2009]). Shane argues persuasively that we have not realized how much the medium really does determine the message (ala Marshall McLuhan). We have missed the fact that the move from orality/aurality to writing/reading shapes what happens cognitively and shows that we inhabit the message in a different way.
2. I am not diminishing the importance of the gift of teaching in the body of Christ. I am suggesting, however, that we have created dependence on the teacher as the dispenser of all things good (think *shaman* from chapter 8), and as a result we have a community of actors attempting to improv a script they have rarely, if ever, read

in its entirety. What a crazy state of affairs. We have a script, and we are to perform a fifth act in continuity, on a performance trajectory, with these four acts, but we haven't thoroughly read and immersed ourselves in the four acts.

3. The classic is William Isaac's *Dialogue and the Art of Thinking Together* (New York: Broadway Books, 1999). Creating dialogue space for script-ure reading is something that provides an exciting frontier for recapturing the idea of *coming to know together*. Other resources include David Bohm, *On Dialogue* (2d ed.; New York: Routledge, 2004); Robert Apatow, *The Art of Spiritual Dialogue* (Rochester, Vt.: Inner Traditions, 1998); Daniel Yankelovich, *The Magic of Dialogue* (New York: Touchstone, 2001).

4. Several weeks earlier, our group had watched an hour-long interview with Ray Kurzweil on his theory of singularity in which he talked about this issue of computer/brain computing speed.

5. In addition to Margaret Wheatley's writings, see Juanita Brown, *The World Café: Shaping Our Future Through Conversations That Matter* (San Francisco: Berrett-Koehler, 2005). The concept of World Café is interesting in its own right, but I am more interested in what we can learn from the model of facilitation she and others practice.

Chapter 14: The Role of Other Actors

1. Quoted in Wade Baskin, *Classics in Education* (New York: Philosophical Library, 1966), 544.

2. Alfred North Whitehead, *The Aims of Education and Other Essays* (1929; repr., New York: Simon and Schuster, 1967), 1.

3. Tobin Hart, *From Information to Transformation* (New York: Peter Lang, 2000), 16–17.

4. Ibid., 87–115.

5. See Sonia Moore, *The Stanislavski System: The Professional Training of an Actor* (2d rev. ed.; New York: Penguin, 1984). An overview of Stanislavski's system can be found at *http://en.wikipedia.org/wiki/ Stanislavski_Method* (accessed April 15, 2009).

6. Constantin Stanislavski, *An Actor Prepares* (New York: Routledge, 1964), 31.

7. Ibid., 285.
8. Martin Buber, *I and Thou* (1923; repr., New York: Scribner, 1958), 11.
9. Quoted in Kevin Roberts, *Lovemarks* (New York: Powerhouse, 2004), 42.
10. Daniel Goleman's several books on emotional and social intelligence take this as a starting point for understanding human interactions and how we manage our lives.

Chapter 15: Working Examples

1. I would love to see a host of resources developed that could help us in this pursuit. Some resources might simply take some of what is already available in the world of scholarship and make it more accessible. It might also mean, though, that new resources will need to be crafted that take seriously the script and its basis for improv.
2. See, for example, Romans 5:12–19; 1 Corinthians 15:2–49. See James Dunn, *Christology in the Making: An Inquiry into the Origins of the Doctrine of the Incarnation* (2d ed.; London: SCM Press, 1989).
3. See Exodus 15:24; 16:2, 7 (2x), 8 (3x), 9, 12; 17:3; Numbers 14:2, 27 (3x), 29, 36; 16:11, 41; 17:5 (2x), 10. For more thoughts on this connection, see Bruce Malina and Jon Pilch, *Social-Science Commentary on the Letters of Paul* (Minneapolis: Augsburg, 2006), 307.
4. Malina and Pilch, *Social-Science Commentary*, 306.

DISCUSSION QUESTIONS

CHAPTER 1: My First Experience

1. All of our initial experiences with the Bible are formative in some way. What was yours like? If it was a childhood experience, what do you remember about it? Who was it with? What church was it in? What feelings do you have? If your experience with the Bible came later in life, what were the circumstance surrounding that encounter?

2. What stories, passages, or even Sunday school teachers, pastors, priests, or catechism classes are etched in your mind?

3. Looking back, how were those initial experiences building blocks for your thoughts and attitudes toward the Bible that you still carry today? Are they generally positive or negative?

CHAPTER 2: The Tattoo Incident

1. Those first run-ins with the text—where things don't add up, details don't make sense, everything isn't neat and tidy—can be disorienting and even upsetting moments. What are your first "tattoo incident" experiences? Where did they happen? Was it in a group meeting, during a sermon you heard, as you did your own personal Bible reading? What was the text? What did you feel?

2. What did you do with the feelings of disorientation? Did they ever get resolved? Did you go to a parent, a teacher, a friend? Did you bury the inconsistencies and file them in a question bin in the back of your mind?

3. What did these run-ins with the text do to your confidence in the Bible and in God? How did it affect your ability to trust?

CHAPTER 3: Presbyterian, Catholic, and Charismatic

1. The tradition(s) to which we are first exposed deeply impact the way we touch, feel, and experience the biblical world. What was your tradition? What sort of home did you grow up in—Catholic, Presbyterian, Baptist, Pentecostal, non-denominational, agnostic, or ... ?

2. In this chapter, I use the metaphor of lenses for the ways we see the Bible—ways that may be tacit or hidden from our conscious view. When did you first become aware you had lenses? As your journey has progressed, describe how you have been able to identify the lenses you have inherited.

3. When it first dawns on us that we are wearing lenses, we

often experience the shock of finding out that we have not been seeing the 100 percent clear, objective, obvious truth of the Bible we always assumed it had. In other words, we realize we don't see it all. How did that impact your relationship to the Bible and to God? What feelings surrounded that dawning?

4. Two haunting ruminations are mentioned in this chapter. What are yours? Do you have any nagging, unresolved questions that are intruding at the forefront of your mind?

CHAPTER 4: Basic Instructions Before Leaving Earth

1. One of the groups in which I was growing spiritually had specific lenses related to "the end times" — that is, what is going to happen before Jesus returns. Almost everything in the Bible can be fit into something related to this framing story of the end times. These were strong prescription lenses. There was a whole theological world you "saw" when you wore these lenses. What "world" were you in as you realized you had on a pair of glasses? Was it the world of liturgical worship, fundamentalist rule keeping, charismatic prophetic expression? What did the sermons you heard center on? What stands out as most memorable?

2. How did that world frame, inform, or even marinade the way you read the Bible? How did those memorable messages subtly influence your daily Bible reading?

CHAPTER 5: Selective Application

1. There are many examples in which a "pick and choose what applies and what doesn't apply" situation occurs? As you read this chapter, were there specific Bible passages that came to mind? Can you recall discussions, even debates, in which the issue was about why one part of a passage applied and another part of the same passage didn't? What were the passages? What was the outcome of the conversations?

2. As you read this chapter, what feelings did you have as you thought about biblical stories such as Nicodemus and the rich young ruler and the applications that are often given to these stories?

CHAPTER 6: The Guiding Question Crystallized

1. As you have read the Bible, what has been your dominant framing question? Or put another way, when you are reading the Bible, what are you hoping or expecting to find? What are you looking for? This is a revealing question — a question that reveals the lenses we are wearing but might not realize we are wearing.

2. How have you decided what applies and what doesn't as you read the Bible? For instance, when you read about God's instructions to Noah to build an ark, you probably didn't conclude this is a command to you to build an ark. When you read that God had a plan for Jeremiah's life, you probably assumed God has a plan for your life as well. What makes one of those "obviously" apply and the other not?

3. What do you think of the idea that the question we have been asking is inadequate and that a new question is needed? Do you agree? Why or why not?

4. What new questions do you think we should be asking? What do you think of the new question proposed in this chapter?

CHAPTER 7: Faith and Human Development

1. Most of us love personality profiles, self-scoring tests, strength identifiers, categories we can insert ourselves into so that we will better understand our journey. What did you learn about human development in this chapter? What feelings were being stirred up inside of you as you read?

2. What do you think of the idea of faith development? Does it encourage you? Does it help you understand the role of doubt and disruption in the process of experiencing growth in our faith? Which of the categories would you place yourself in at this point in your life?

3. How has this tool of human development helped you see how your understanding of and relationship to the Bible may change as you go through various growth stages? Is this helpful, threatening, disconcerting, exhilarating, or ...?

4. This chapter introduces the concept of liminal space, the in-between spaces of life in which we are moving from one place to another but haven't quite completed the move. Where have you experienced liminal space in your faith journey? Where are you experiencing it now?

5. The *certainty value* is huge in our culture — and nearly as big in our church culture. How are you doing in navigating the

uncertainties of life? What impact does this struggle with certainty/uncertainty have on your relationship with God and with the Bible?

CHAPTER 8: View of God/View of Scripture

1. Think back to your earliest exposure to God and the Bible. Which do you remember first — Bible stories, or talking to or hearing about God? Was it the Bible that introduced you to God first? Or was it God whom you knew, and then the Bible became a window through which you learned more about him and grew to love and trust him more?

2. If you grew up in a faith community, can you articulate how its view of God and the Bible was mutually reinforcing? For instance, if the Bible is a rule book for life, then surely the rule giver is God, who is trying to make sure we play by the rules. What was your experience of the dance of knowing God and understanding the Bible?

3. What do you think of my friend Joe's idea that pastors are modern-day shamans — brokers of the truth of God, gurus with answers to all your questions?

CHAPTER 9: Shifting Our View of the Bible

1. What did you find most challenging about this chapter?

2. Is the idea of cultural evolution and its application to various biblical texts a helpful way of encouraging new understandings? What aha moments did you have as you read about this?

3. What passages and stories, when viewed through the lens of cultural evolution, could mean something far different than what you may have been taught?

4. If God isn't changing, but humans are progressing in their understanding of the world, God, and each other, what are the implications for future understandings of God?

5. What dominant metaphors have you had concerning the Bible? How have they been helpful in serving a purpose? Are they still effective, or are new ones needed?

CHAPTER 10: New Metaphors for the Shift

1. How has your dominant metaphor been a filter or guide in determining what you are reading and looking for?

2. Of the two metaphors in this chapter—Bible as a classic or a jazz score—which one most resonated with you? What did you find helpful about it?

3. If you are using this book for group study, you may want to read the book of Jonah and look at it through a new set of lenses and see a new thing together as a group. Describe some of the findings that have been the most surprising as you do this exercise together.

4. The jazz score metaphor is built around the idea of community interaction. How is this picture of relating in a community helpful when it comes to interpreting the biblical text?

CHAPTER 11: The Drama Script

1. What happens if you approach the Bible more as a drama script than as an owner's manual for life? How does this technique change what you look for and see?
2. What is your growing sense of the large sweep of the biblical story? Try to summarize in a paragraph what this sweeping story line is. What would it be like in the context of community to develop an ongoing and constantly updating narrative line for each book in the Bible and for the whole of the Bible?

CHAPTER 12: Immersing in the First Four Acts

1. Find a group of people with whom you can begin the "read-through" practice. Pick a small Bible book, and read the entire book in one sitting out loud, allowing various people to read. Ignore chapter and verse divisions. Read it as a story.
2. What happens as you read out loud? What do you hear in this communal reading that you have missed in the past when you read it to yourself? What do you hear differently as different people are reading? Where have you been experiencing inattentional blindness?
3. As you read aloud, what are you coming to know *together* that is different from what you discover as you read alone?

CHAPTER 13: The Role of the "Acting Community"

1. This chapter has a list of questions in the middle of it. As a group, take these questions and talk about them. This may be the first time that many people have heard large blocks of the Bible read out loud.

2. Start creating a wiki-synthesis for the book you are reading aloud—an open-source, updatable, shared understanding of the book's narrative sweep. What are people hearing?

3. Laying the groundwork for dialogue may be a necessary starting point for some groups. Depending on the level of trust and openness to observations from various group members, it might be good to start with the concept and help people learn to suspend judgment and redirect their attention through asking good questions.

CHAPTER 14: The Role of Other Actors

1. What kinds of questions came to mind as you reflected on the stages that information moves through to get to transformation? As you ponder where you are in this continuum, which stage has dominated your life? How would you describe the stage at which most of your Christian training and Bible study has occurred?

2. What do you think the role of the Holy Spirit is in the context of community? How do community consensus and the voice of the Holy Spirit interact? Do we all need to see things the same? How do you feel about dissenting opinions? How important is it that we are all on the same page?

CHAPTER 15: Working Examples

1. This chapter points us to the book of Philippians. I suggest that you read chapter 15 together in a group and pause when prompted so you can read the book of Philippians out loud. Then engage the questions from chapter 13. Create your own wiki-synthesis of the book. Enjoy!

Transformational Architecture

Reshaping Our Lives as Narrative

Ron Martoia

"How Can I More Effectively Reach People of My Generation with the Message of the Gospel?"

Start the story where God starts the story.

In other words, it's not about "lifestyle evangelism." Or being cleverer than the person with whom you're talking. Or knowing everything there is to know about the Bible.

It's about knowing what's most important to your friends, family, coworkers, and others you meet along life's journey. It's about, to use author Ron Martoia's words, discovering the "story" each of us lives every waking day of our lives. Once you know that, you'll know how God's story fits into our human stories.

Jesus spread the Good News this way. He talked to people, asked them questions about who they were, what they were doing—in short, he found out what made each person get out of bed every morning. And then he shared with them a bigger story—and how they fit into it. Jesus knew that when people grasped God's big picture, they felt compelled—even overjoyed—to be a part of it.

In today's increasingly individualistic, disenfranchised world, it's never been more important to know God's story and how one fits into it. Let *Transformational Architecture* be your guide to reaching those around you with God's life-changing message of hope.

Softcover: 978-0-310-28769-8

Share Your Thoughts

With the Author: Your comments will be forwarded to
the author when you send them to *zauthor@zondervan.com*.

With Zondervan: Submit your review of this book
by writing to *zreview@zondervan.com*.

Free Online Resources at
www.zondervan.com

Zondervan AuthorTracker: Be notified whenever your favorite
authors publish new books, go on tour, or post an update
about what's happening in their lives at www.zondervan.com/
authortracker.

Daily Bible Verses and Devotions: Enrich your life with daily
Bible verses or devotions that help you start every morning
focused on God. Visit www.zondervan.com/newsletters.

Free Email Publications: Sign up for newsletters on Christian
living, academic resources, church ministry, fiction, children's
resources, and more. Visit www.zondervan.com/newsletters.

Zondervan Bible Search: Find and compare Bible passages in
a variety of translations at www.zondervanbiblesearch.com.

Other Benefits: Register yourself to receive online benefits
like coupons and special offers, or to participate in research.

ZONDERVAN®

ZONDERVAN.com/
AUTHORTRACKER
follow your favorite authors